The French in the Americas,
1620-1820

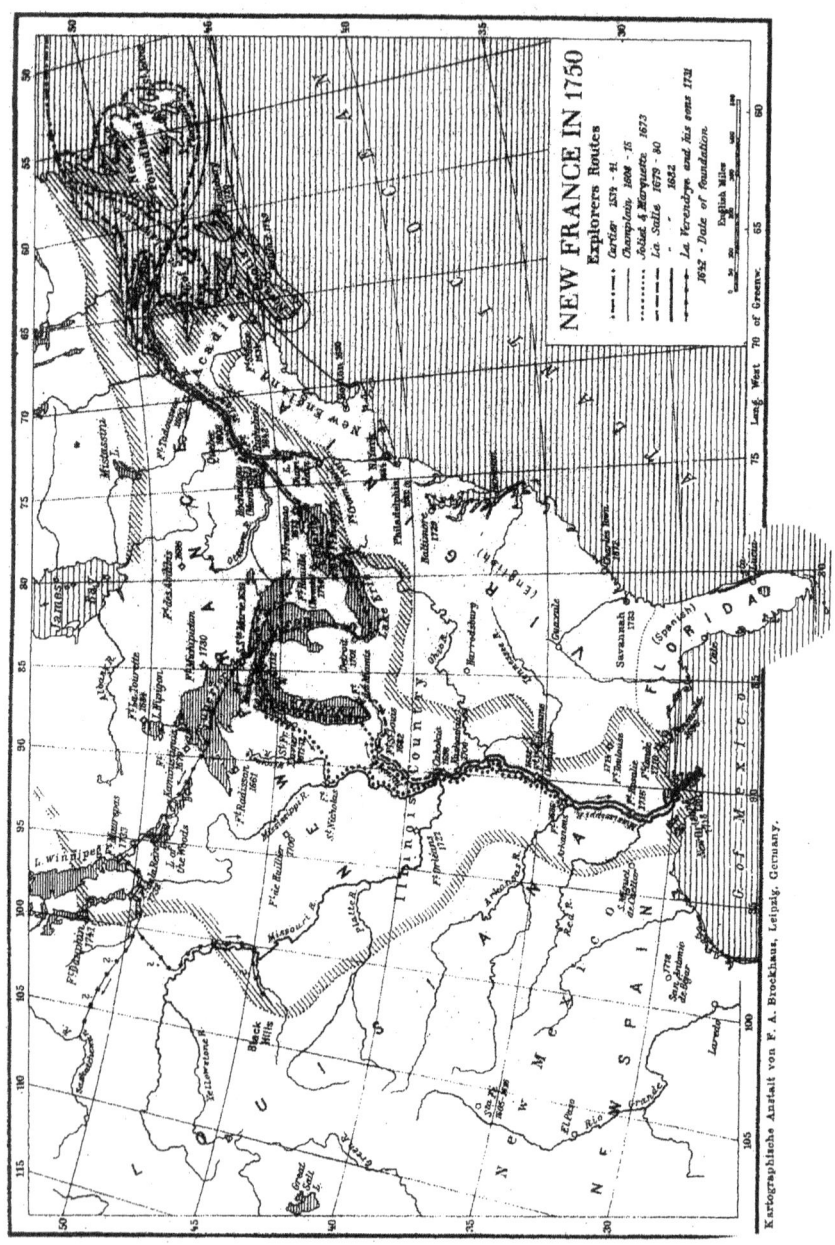

The French in the Americas,

1620-1820

By
David Dobson

Copyright © 2011
by David Dobson
All Rights Reserved

Printed for Clearfield Company by
Genealogical Publishing Company
Baltimore, Maryland
2011

ISBN 978-0-8063-5546-7

Made in the United States of America

INTRODUCTION

French attempts at establishing colonies in the Americas date from the early sixteenth century. In the 1530s Jacques Cartier explored the St Lawrence River and in 1541 established a colony at Charlesbourg-Royal. During 1555 French Huguenots attempted to form a settlement on the coast of Brazil, which was destroyed by the Portuguese in 1560. Within a few years two Huguenot colonies were founded on the North American mainland, one at Charlesfort, a site in present day South Carolina, and the other at Fort Caroline in Florida, both were soon eliminated by the Spanish who had a prior claim to the region.

During the seventeenth century the emphasis of French settlement in the Americas was in Acadia, also in Canada which extended through the American Mid-West to Louisiana, along with various islands in the Antilles and St Dominigue. By the middle of the eighteenth century an estimated 15,000 colonists lived in Acadia, 55,000 in Canada, with 10,000 in Louisiana and Illinois. In the Caribbean the main French settlements were Guadaloupe, Martinique, Cayenne, and St Dominique with a population, mainly of French and African origin, amounting to around 250,000. Within the British colonies in America and the West Indies there was a significant number of French Protestants or Huguenots. Who were the French colonists of early America, the ancestors of thousands of present day Canadians and Americans? While the main sources of information on this may lie in French or North American archives there is some material in British archives. This publication is designed to identify people of French origin in the Americas largely based on documents found in British government records.

David Dobson

Dundee, Scotland, 2011

The French in the Americas, 1620-1820

SOURCES

APCCol		Acts of the Privy Council, Colonial, series
BN	=	Bibliotheque Nationale, Paris
CalHOP		Calendar of Home Office Papers, series
CLRO	=	City of London Record Office
CSPC	=	Calendar of State Papers, Colonial, series
FPA	=	The Fulham Papers in the Lambeth Library, Oxford, 1965
GAR	=	Rotterdam Archives
HCF	=	Histoire de Colonies Francaises, Paris, 1929
HLF	=	Histoire e la Louisiane Francaise, Paris, 1994
HMC	=	Historical Manuscripts Commission
JCTP	=	Journal of the Commissioners for Trade and Plantations, series
LIS	=	List and Index Society, London
NA	=	National Archives, London
NRS	=	National Archives of Scotland, Edinburgh
PCC	=	Prerogative Court of Canterbury
SM	=	Scots Magazine, series
SPAWI	=	State Papers, America and the West Indies, series

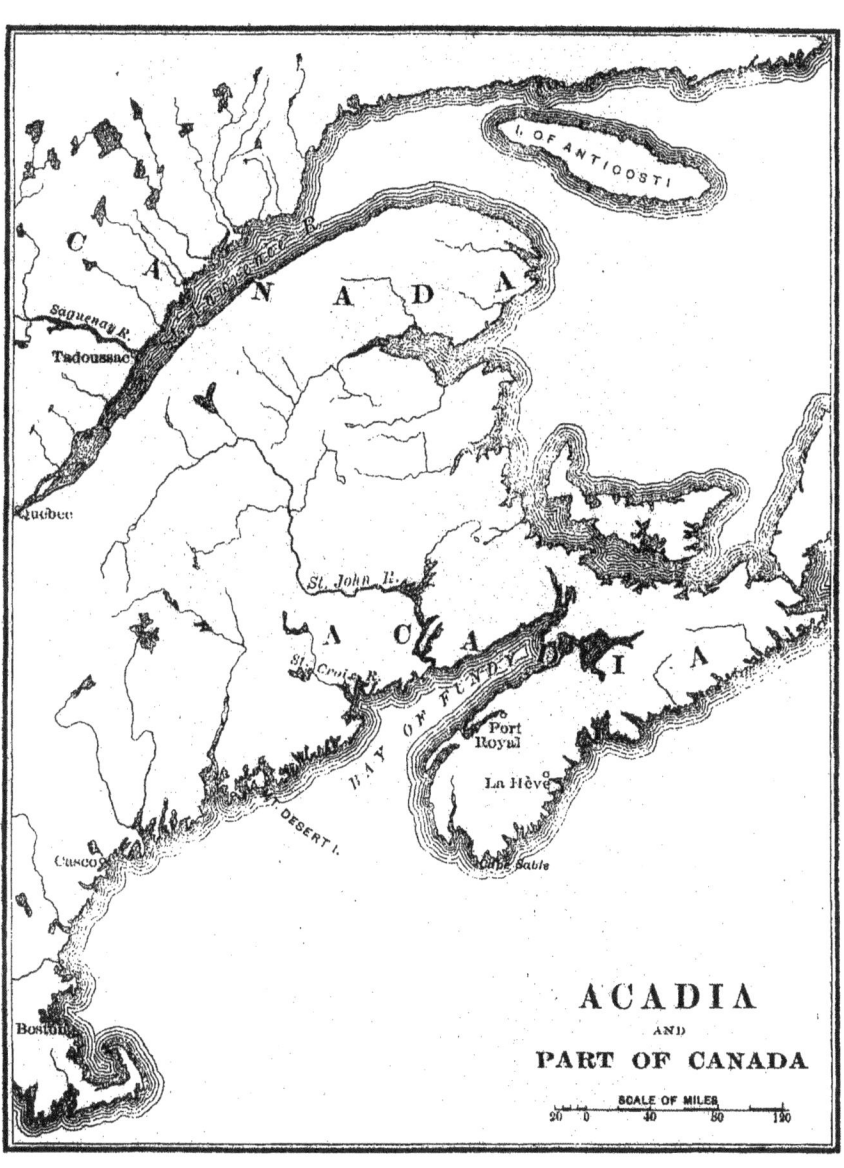

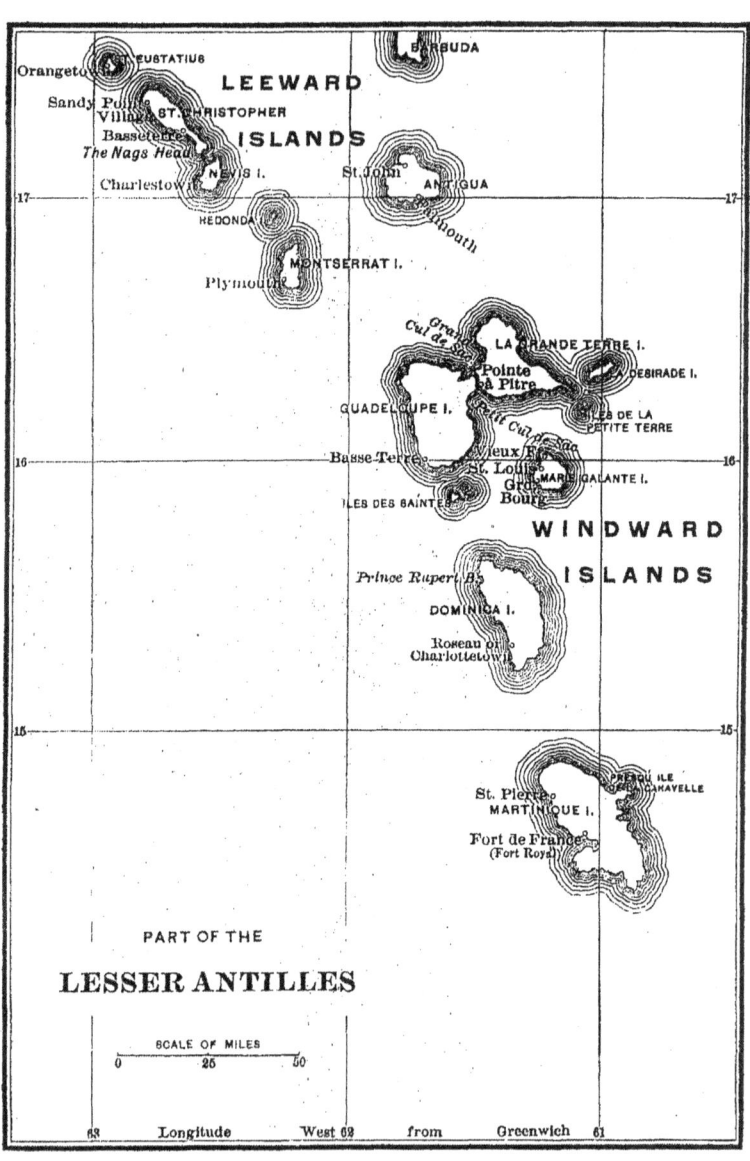

The French in the Americas, 1620-1820

ABRARD, ELIE, master of the L'Armes de France from La Rochelle to Canada and the West Indies in 1684. [Charente Maritime Archives]

ACHARD, MICHEL, master of La Belle Madelon from La Rochelle to the West Indies and Acadia in 1684. [Charente Maritime Archives]

AEREAUD, PIERRE, master of the Saint Louis de la Rochelle from La Rochelle to Quebec and the West Indies in 1699. [La Rochelle Archives]

ALBANAL, ..., a priest at Hudson Bay, 1670s. [SPAWI.1684.2097]

ALLAIN, LOUIS, at Port Royal, Quebec, 1718. [SPAWI.1718.789iii]

ALLART, CAROUCH, Captain, master of Le Juste at Martinique in 1702. [SPAWI.1702.195]

AMBLAND, PIERRE, master of Le Bien Aime de Bordeaux which was captured when bound for Quebec in 1748. [NA.HCA32.99/2]

AMITT, ..., in Quebec, 1765. [JCTP.Vol.72.224]

AMYAND, ISAAC, was granted 200 acres in Craven County, South Carolina, 1737. [NA.CO5.398]

ANGELIERE, ELIZABETH, a French refugee, landed in Virginia, 1700. [SPAWI.1700.681]

ANGIER, SUSANNA, in Kingston, Jamaica, and her daughters Mary and Frances, 1741. [APCCol.][JCTP.1741.379]

ANGIER, ..., in St Kitts, 1672. [SPAWI.1672.903]

ANGLOSERY, ..., Lieutenant Governor of Quebec, 1708. [SPAWI.1708.60]

ARAMY, LOUIS, master of the Recontre de la Rochelle from France to Quebec and the West Indies in 1698. [Gironde Archives, 6BB73.66/6B294]

ARCENEAU, PETER, a voyage from Baubassin to Cape Gaspe, 1714. [JCTP.1715.71][SPAWI.1715.568v]

The French in the Americas, 1620-1820

ARDENAY, ANDRE, from Sabel D'Olone, France, bound for Newfoundland aboard the St Anna, master Jacques Fevre, 1640. [GAR.ONA.169.78.123; 431.62.81]

ARNAUD, ISAAC, and wife, French refugees, landed in Virginia, 1700. [SPAWI.1700.681]

ARNAUD, JACQUES, master of the Saint Simon de Bordeaux from Bordeaux to Quebec in 1672 and in 1673. [Bordeaux Archives, Ferrand.151/1243]

ARNAUD, VEUVE ANTOINE, in St Vincent's, 1777. [JCTP.84.69]

ARNAUD, Captain, from France to Canada, 1630. [CSPC.V.80]

ARNAULT, THOMAS CHABAUD, in Dominica, 1772. [JCTP.1772.319]

ARTELL, ..., near Shamblee, Quebec, 1711; commandant of troops at Cape Breton, 1713. [JCTP.1711.673][SPAWI.1713.522]

ASSAILIES, KATHERINE, daughter of Peter Assailies in St Kitts, 1720. [APCCol.1720.1225]

ASSAILIES, MARTHA, daughter of Peter Assaillies, a Huguenot and planter, who to escape religious persecution in French St Kitts fled to Boston, New England, before 1695; estates restored in 1715; 1716. [APCCol.1715.1225][SPAWI.1714.630xvi; 1715.375; 1716.134/173]

ASSAILLIE, Mrs, in St Kitts, 1717. [JCTP.1717.208]

AUBODON, JOHN JAMES, born 1774 in New Orleans, a naturalist who died in New York on 27 January 1851. [GM.NS35.440]

AUBOYNEAU, ..., in Connecticut or Rhode Island, 1706. [JCTP.1706.221/243]

AUDOUY, ABRAHAM, a French Protestant, petitioned to be shipped to America, possibly went to Jamaica, 1682. [SPAWI.1682.883]

AUBOYNEAU, JOHN, in New York, 1703, 1714. [SPAWI.1705.1475xxv; 1714.67iii]

AUBRY, ..., Commandant at New Orleans, 1765. [JCTP.1765.267]

The French in the Americas, 1620-1820

AUDIAN, ISAAC PETER, a planter, and his infant sons Andrew and Peter, in St Kitts, 1722; 1723; 1746. [APCCol.1733-1734][JCTP.1723.28; 1733. 354/365/375/398; 1746.219]

AUDIERE, FRANCOIS, master of Saint Francois de la Rochelle from La Rochelle to Quebec and the West Indies in 1687. [Charente Maritime Archives, B235.139]

AUDIVEI, BARTHOLEMEW, a native of Toulon, in Frederica, Georgia, 1744. [JCTP.1744.130]

AUFFRAY, CLAUDE, senior, in Dominica, 1771. [JCTP.1773.274]

AUFFRAY, CLAUDE, junior, in Dominica, 1771. [JCTP.1773.274]

AUFFRAY, FRANCOIS, in Dominica, 1771. [JCTP.1773.274]

AUGIER, Chevalier, Governor of Mariegalante, 1691. [SPAWI.1691.1557]

AURILLEAU, ZACHARIE, master of Saint Honore de la Rochelle from Bordeaux to Canada in 1687. [Gironde Archives, 6B72/78-81]

AVICE, JOHN, master of the Fleuron de Saint Malo seized by the British at Montserrat, 1736. [SPAWI.1737.61i]

AYGRON, CLAUDE, master of the L'Aimable from La Rochelle to Mississippi on 24 July 1684. [Charente Maritime Archives ms]

AYRAULT, PIERRE, and his son Daniel, in Naragansett, New England, 1700. [SPAWI.1705.1451xxvii/xxviii]

BABY, FRANCIS, Councillor of Quebec, 1777. [JCTP.Vol.84.106]

BADOUET, ESTIENNE, a French refugee, landed in Virginia, 1700. [SPAWI.1700.681]

BAGON, ..., Intendant of Canada, 1722. [SPAWI.1723.805]

BAILLAIRGE, Sieur JEAN, a master builder in Quebec, witness to a Loyalist claim, 1786. [NA.AO13.24.136-143]

The French in the Americas, 1620-1820

BAILLERGEAU, JACOB, a French Protestant, petitioned to be shipped to America, possibly went to Jamaica, 1682. [SPAWI.1682.883]

BALAGUIER, JOHN, deputy secretary of St Kitts, 1725. [SPAWI.1725.648ii]

BAPTIST, JEAN, in Dominica, 1771. [JCTP.1773.248]

BARBE, ADRIAN, a Walloon dyer, with his wife and four children, to emigrate to Virginia, 1621. [CSPC.Addenda; Colonial Correspondence, Vol.i,#45]

BARBOUTTAIN, JOHN, a gentleman in Antigua, 1709, deceased by 1728. [SPAWI.1709.487ii][APCCol.1729.177]

BARDEN, CLAUD, and wife, French refugees, landed in Virginia, 1700. [SPAWI.1700.681]

BARJAUT, JEAN, master of the Fleur de Lys from France to Quebec in 1688. [Gironde Archives, 6B72/60]

BARNARD, DAVID, a French refugee, landed in Virginia, 1700. [SPAWI.1700.681]

BARTOUILH, DOMINIQUE, in Dominica, 1773. [JCTP.1773.334]

BASSOU, JEAN, a French refugee, landed in Virginia, 1700. [SPAWI.1700.681]

BATAILLE, PIERRE, master of Saint Pierre de la Rochelle from La Rochelle to Quebec in 1679; master of Saint Antoine de la Rochelle from Bordeaux to Quebec in 1685. [Charente Maritime Archives, B5678; Gironde Archives, 6B71.64, 6B291]

BAYEAUX, THOMAS, in New York, co-owner of the Rhode Island built sloop Good Intent, 1717. [JCTP.1717.437]

BEAUBOIS, CROQUET, in Dominica, 1771. [JCTP.1773.274]

BEAUJEAU, ..., master of the Joly from La Rochelle bound for the Mississippi on 24 July 1684. [Bibliotheque Nationale, Collection Clairambault, 1015/387]

BEAULIEU, HENRY, in Antigua, 1709. [SPAWI.1709.487ii]

The French in the Americas, 1620-1820

BEAUMONT, GILES, a Frenchman denizised for England and Virginia, authorised to take a group of men to Virginia, 31 December 1624. [CSPCol.III.28/31]

BEAUREGARD, ..., Governor of St Domingo, 1699. [SPAWI.1699.45]

BEAU-SOLEIL, ..., a soldier, killed by the Chicachas at Fort Saint Claude in 1730. [HLF]

BEAVA, GEORGE, a porter, with his wife and one child, to emigrate to Virginia, 1621. [CSPC.Addenda; Colonial Correspondence, Vol.i,#45]

BEGON, Chevalier, French Intendant at Quebec, 1714; Major of the Town, Castle, and Government of Quebec, 1727. [SPAWI.1714.280; 1727.684]

BELAIN, PIERRE, master of La Catholique from Le Havre to St Kitts and Barbados on 24 February 1627. [HCF.I.392]

BELAVENE, ..., to recruit ten or twelve men for Carolina, 1630. [CSPCol.V]

BELELL, ..., in Nova Scotia, 1711. [JCTP.1711.673]

BELLAIR, CHARLES MARTIN ROGER, in Dominica, 1775, 1776. [JCTP.1775.441; 1776.13]

BELLAIR, FRANCIS ROGER, in Dominica, 1772. [JCTP.1772.319; 1775.441; 1776.13]

BELLAIR, ROGER, in Dominica, 1772. [JCTP.1772.319]

BELLEFEVIELL, ..., in Placentia, Newfoundland, 1703. [SPAWI.1704.315h]

BELLEFONTAINE, Le Sieur, a settler on the River St John, Acadia, 1715. [SPAWI.1715.142iv]

BELLENGER, WILLIAM, in South Carolina, 1724; was granted 1200 acres in Granville County, South Carolina, 1738. [SPAWI.1724.388i][NA.CO5.398]

BELLISLE, ..., in Quebec, 1723. [SPAWI.1723.805]

BENESTEAU, JEAN, master of St Louis from Bordeaux to Quebec and the West Indies in 1695. [Bordeaux Archives]

The French in the Americas, 1620-1820

BENESTEAU, SALOMON, master of St Louis from Bordeaux to Quebec and the West Indies in 1695. [Charente Maritime Archives, B235/273/336]

BENOIST, PETER, was granted 341 acres in Craven County, South Carolina, 1738. [NA.CO5.398]

BERNARD, DANIEL, a French Protestant, petitioned to be shipped to America, possibly went to Jamaica, 1682. [SPAWI.1682.883]

BERNARD, ELIAS, was granted 200 acres in Granville County, South Carolina, 1738. [NA.CO5.398]

BERNOE, …….., a gentleman in Curacao, January 1709. [SPAWI.1709.411ii]

BERNON, GABRIEL, a planter in New Oxford, New England, and in Boston, 1696; in Rhode Island, a petition, 1699.[SPAWI.1696.514/533; 1699.890xix]

BERTHOUMIEU, BERTRAND, master of La Marie Ester which was captured when bound from the West Indies in 1745. [NA.HCA32.131/2]

BERTRAN, PIERRE, master of Le Redoubtable, a privateer, which was captured when bound from the West Indies in 1744. [NA.HCA32.150]

BERTRAND, FRANCIS, born in La Rochelle, a ship's carpenter aboard the Anne and Katherine, from New York via Maryland bound for London in 1690. [NA.HCA.Rex v. The Anne and Katherine, 1692]

BESSE, JEAN, master of Le Vigillant which was captured when bound from the West Indies in 1748. [NA.HCA32.156/1]

BEUSE, CHARLES, in St Vincent, 1773. [JCTP.1773.334]

BEUSE, JEAN, in St Vincent, 1773. [JCTP.1773.334]

BEUSE, PHILIP, in St Vincent, 1773. [JCTP.1773.334]

BIEUVILLE, M., Governor of Moville, 1736. [SPAWI.1736.381]

BIGNION, JOSEPH, was granted 1000 acres in Granville County, South Carolina, 1738. [NA.CO5.398]

The French in the Americas, 1620-1820

BIGOT, JACQUES, master of La Genevieve a privateer which was captured when bound for the West Indies in 1748. [NA.HCA32.114]

BILBEAU, JACQUES, a French refugee, landed in Virginia, 1700. [SPAWI.1700.681]

BILBOT, FRANCOIS, a French refugee, landed in Virginia, 1700. [SPAWI.1700.681]

BILLOT, CATHARINE, a French refugee, landed in Virginia, 1700. [SPAWI.1700.681]

BILLOUARD DE KERLEREC, Le Chevalier LOUIS, Governor of Louisiana, 1753. [HLF]

BILLOUIN, HONNORE LOUIS, master of L'Intriguant which was captured when bound from the West Indies in 1744. [NA.HCA32.118/1]

BIORET, JACQUES, wife and two children, French refugees, landed in Virginia, 1700. [SPAWI.1700.681]

BISROULL, PIERRE, in Rhode Island, a petition, 1699.[SPAWI.1699.890xix]

BLAETRAN, NICOLAS, master of La Notre Dame de Possession de la Rochelle from France to Quebec in 1691, seized and landed in Boston. [La Rochelle Archives, Riviere/Soulard mss]

BLENAC, Count, Governor of Martinique, 1686. [SPAWI.1730.324]

BLINART, M., later a General, who led the French invasion of Tobago, 1676. [SPAWI.1677.559]

BLONDEL, ..., in Martinique, 1724. [SPAWI.1724.400ii]

BODETT, ..., in St Kitts, 1672. [SPAWI.1672.903]

BOFFE, FRANCOIS, a French refugee, landed in Virginia, 1700. [SPAWI.1700.681]

BOICEAU, ..., a minister bound for Virginia, 1689. [SPAWI.1689.670]

The French in the Americas, 1620-1820

BOINEAU, MICHAEL, guilty of murdering Captain Peter Simmons, in South Carolina, 1724. [SPAWI.1724.388v]

BOIREAU, JOHN, in Frederica, Georgia, 1744. [JCTP.1744.130]

BOIS, PIERRE, a merchant at Canso, Canada, 1719. [SPAWI.1719.208ii]

BOISNELLE, SIMON, and family, settled in Highgate, Georgia, dead by 1737. [NA.CO5.145/145D]

BOISSEAU, JAMES, a clergyman in Virginia, 1705. [SPAWI.1705.924i]

BOISSEAU, PIERRE, master of La Catherine which was captured when bound from the West Indies in 1745 or 1746. [NA.HCA32.101/1]

BOISSEAU, ..., in Quebec, 1765. [JCTP.Vol.72.224]

BOMARD, CATHARINE, a French refugee, landed in Virginia, 1700. [SPAWI.1700.681]

BOMBRON, Captain, master of Le Modere at Martinique in 1702. [SPAWI.1702.195]

BON, LOUIS, a French refugee, landed in Virginia, 1700. [SPAWI.1700.681]

BONALL, ANTHONY, residing at Buck Row, Virginia, 1624

BONAMI, GERMAIN, master of L'Europe which was captured when bound from the West Indies in 1747. [NA.HCA32.107/1]

BONAMI, Madame, on St Vincent, 1767. [JCTP.1767.283]

BONAVENTURE, ..., a French officer, from Cape Breton to Boston, New England, 1714. [SPAWI.1715.568iii]

BONDINOT, MAGDALEN, widow and executrix of John Bondinot of Antigua, 1725. [APCCol.1725.87]

BONFILS, JEAN, master of Les Deux Freres de Bordeaux from France to Quebec in 1695. [Gironde Archives, 6B76.103.117]

BONFILS, JOHN, a French subject, trading in or with Jamaica from the Amiable Mary, 1716. [APCCol.1725.80]

The French in the Americas, 1620-1820

BONFILS, PETER, a French subject, trading in or with Jamaica from L'Amiable Marie, 1716. [APCCol.1725.80][SPAWI.1719.167.i]

BONNEAU, ANTHONY, in South Carolina, 1724. [SPAWI.1724.388i]

BONNEAU, HENRY, was granted 500 acres on the Pon Pon River, and 131 acres in Berkley County, South Carolina, 1737. [NA.CO5.398]

BONNEMERE, ..., a French Protestant in St Kitts, 1672/1673; 1690. [SPAWI.1672.903; 1673.1048; 1674.1273; 1690.1212]

BONNIN, GOUSSE, in Antigua, 1709. [SPAWI.1709.487ii]

BONNINGER, ABRAHAM, was granted 200 acres in Granville County, South Carolina, 1738. [NA.CO5.398]

BONOVRIER, ISAAC, a deposition re the Newfoundland salmon fishery, 8 August 1720. [SPAWI.1720.335vi]

BONTAU, JACQUES, master of Anne de Nantes a privateer which was captured when bound from the West Indies in 1745. [NA.HCA32.94/1]

BONTINAN, DOROTHY, in St Anne's, Sandy Point, St Kitts, 1724. [APCCol.1727.135]

BONVERON, SIMEON, in Montserrat, 1733,1737. [SPAWI.1733.446; 1737.55]

BONYOE, ISAAC, was granted 150 acres in Granville County, South Carolina, 1738. [NA.CO5.398]

BORTRO, PIERRE, a planter at Corbin, Placentia Bay, Newfoundland, 1727, 1728. [SPAWI.1727.721][JCTP.1728.395]

BORVELIO, ROBERT, master of the shalop St Dominique seized at Montserrat, 1736. [SPAWI.1737.61i]

BOUCHETT, ..., a French refugee, landed in Virginia, 1700. [SPAWI.1700.681]

BOUDET, MICHEL, in Newfoundland, 1731. [SPAWI.1731.422]

BOUDEWYNE, JOHN, master of the schooner Prosperity seized at Montserrat, 1736. [SPAWI.1737.61i]

The French in the Americas, 1620-1820

BOUDINOT, JOHN, a merchant and planter in Antigua, 1718. [SPAWI.1718.413]

BOUDROT, MICHEL, at Les Mines, Nova Scotia, 1732. [SPAWI.1732.152]

BOULAY, ..., Governor of St Domingo, 1705. [JCTP.1706.306]

BOURDENAUX, M. from Jamaica aboard the Adventure of London, bound, via England, for France, 1670. [SPAWI.167-.174]

BOURDET, ISAAC, a French refugee, landed in Virginia, 1700. [SPAWI.1700.681]

BOURDON DOMBOURG, J.F., master of the St Francois Xavier de Quebec from La Rochelle to Quebec in 1680. [Charente Maritime Archives, B5679]

BOUREAU, JAMES ANDREW, was aboard the privateer Benjamin when it was captured when bound from the West Indies in 1744. [NA.HCA.32.98/4]

BOURG, ABRAHAM alias ABRANT, a French inhabitant at the Annapolis River, 1720; at River, Nova Scotia, 1727. [SPAWI.1720.180xvii; 1727.789]

BOURG, ALEXANDER, the King's Procurator in Menis, Nova Scotia, 1732. [SPAWI.1732.153/455]

BOURGEOIS, J., at River, Nova Scotia, 1727. [SPAWI.1727.789]

BOURGOIAN, JOSEPH, a French refugee, landed in Virginia, 1700. [SPAWI.1700.681]

BOURGUIGNON, ..., a soldier, killed by the Chicachas at Fort Saint Claude in 1730. [HLF]

BOURGUIN, BENEDICT, was granted 200 acres in Granville County, South Carolina, 1738. [NA.CO5.398]

BOURGUIN, HENRY, was granted 50 acres in Granville County, South Carolina, 1738. [NA.CO5.398]

BOURGUIN, JOHN BAPTISTE, was granted 100 acres in Granville County, South Carolina, 1738. [NA.CO5.398]

The French in the Americas, 1620-1820

BOURGUIN, MARY, was granted 50 acres in Granville County, South Carolina, 1738. [NA.CO5.398]

BOURRIE, JEAN, a French refugee, landed in Virginia, 1700. [SPAWI.1700.681]

BOURRYEAU, JOHN, in St Kitts, dead by 1729. [SPAWI.1729.908]

BOUYE, JEAN, alleged to have looted a factory at Cape Lopez in the West Indies, 1726. [SPAWI.1726.205]

BOURYAU, JOHN, in St Kitts, 1716, 1733. [JCTP.1716.110][SPAWI.1733.446]

BOYE, JOHN, a Frenchman, soldier in Captain Liston's company, Barbados, 1679.[Brandow's 'Omitted Chapters from Hottens' {Baltimore, 1983}]

BOYNEAU, ..., a French naval commander in the West Indies, 1672. [SPAWI.1672.901]

BRANDS, J., Captain of a Swiss Company of soldiers which mutinied on a voyage from Fort Louis to New Orleans and landed at Charleston, South Carolina, 1722. [SPAWI.1722.372ii]

BREAU, ..., at Cobeguit, Nova Scotia, 1727. [SPAWI.1727.789]

BREBION, PIERRE FRANCOIS EMANUEL, master of <u>La Charlotte</u> which was captured when bound from the West Indies in 1747. [NA.HCA32.102/1]

BRISARD, LOUIS, in Quebec, a deposition, 1763. [JCTP.1763.308]

BRISSON, JACQUES, master of <u>La Champfleur</u> a privateer which was captured when bound from the West Indies around 1746. [NA.HCA102/1]

BROQUE, GILLAIN, a laborer, a young man, to emigrate to Virginia, 1621. [CSPC.Addenda; Colonial Correspondence, Vol.i,#45]

BROQUE, LOUIS, a laborer, with his wife and two children, to emigrate to Virginia, 1621. [CSPC.Addenda; Colonial Correspondence, Vol.i,#45]

BROQUE, ROBERT, a laborer, a young man, to emigrate to Virginia, 1621. [CSPC.Addenda; Colonial Correspondence, Vol.i,#45]

BROUSSE, GABRIEL, in Dominica, 1772. [JCTP.1773.280]

BROUSSE, JACQUES, and child, French refugees, landed in Virginia, 1700. [SPAWI.1700.681]

BROUILLONT, Count, commander at Placentia, Newfoundland, 1697. [SPAWI.1699.793]

BRUCY, ..., at Montreal, 1683. [SPAWI.1683.1201]

BRUYAS, Father J., a Jesuit missionary among the Iroquis, 1699; 1701. [SPAWI.1699.1011xxvii/xxviii; 1701.758]

BUCHE, FRANCIS, was granted 400 acres in Granville County, South Carolina, 1738. [NA.CO5.398]

BUCHES, DAVID, was granted 350 acres in Granville County, South Carolina, 1738. [NA.CO5.398]

BUIGNION, JOSEPH, a Swiss or French minister in Charleston, South Carolina, 1732, in Purrysburg, South Carolina, 1733. [FPA#143/144]; was granted 400 acres in Granville County, South Carolina, 1738. [NA.CO5.398]

BULLT, JAN, a Walloon, a laborer, with his wife and four children, to emigrate to Virginia, 1621. [CSPC.Addenda; Colonial Correspondence, Vol.i,#45]

BUOR, PIERRE, Major in Colonel Alexander's Regiment, a planter in St Kitts, 1726. [SPAWI.1726.236]

CABANIS, HENRY, wife and two children, French refugees, landed in Virginia, 1700. [SPAWI.1700.681]

CABIBEL, PETER, senior, a planter in St Kitts, 1717. [JCTP.1717.260]

CABIBEL, STEPHEN, co-owner of the frigate St Christopher before the Admiralty Court of the Leeward Islands, 3 January 1719. [APCCol.1719.1316]

CAILLAND, ESTIENNE, master of La Junon which was captured when bound from the West Indies in 1744. [NA.HCA32.118/3]

CAILLARD, ANDRE, master of the L'Alexis Bien-aime fishing on the Banks of Newfoundland, 1723. [SPAWI.1723.739iii]

CALANNE, ..., a letter from Quebec, 1756. [JCTP.1757.341]

The French in the Americas, 1620-1820

CAMOUIN, MICHEL, master of the Elizabeth de la Rochelle from France to Quebec in 1698. [Charente Maritime Archives, B5694]

CAMOUIN, MICHEL FRANCOIS, master of the L'Invincible which was captured when bound from the West Indies in 1746. [NA.HCA32.118/1]

CAMPION, JEAN, a wool carder, with his wife and four children, to emigrate to Virginia, 1621. [CSPC.Addenda; Colonial Correspondence, Vol.i,#45]

CAMOUIN, MICHEL FRANCOIS, master of the Benjamin de la Rochelle wich was captured when bound from the West Indies in 1747. [NA.HCA32.99/1]

CAMPION, PHILIPPE, a draper, with his wife and child, to emigrate to Virginia, 1621. [CSPC.Addenda; Colonial Correspondence, Vol.i,#45]

CAMUS, ANDRE, master of Le Saine Jean from La Rochelle to Acadia in 1640. [Charente Maritime Archives, Teuleron,fo.3]

CANDE, MICHEL, master of Louis de la Rochelle, from France to Acadia and Quebec in 1684; from La Rochelle to Acadia in 1685, 1686, and 1687; to Quebec and the West Indies in 1689. [Charente Maritime Archives, B5682/B5685/B235/193; La Rochelle Archives, Berthelot; Gironde Archives, 6B73/132]

CANTAPIE, JEAN, a French refugee, landed in Virginia, 1700. [SPAWI.1700.681]

CANTAPIE, MICHELL, wife and two children, French refugees, landed in Virginia, 1700. [SPAWI.1700.681]

CASSART, ..., led a raid on Montserrat, 1714. [SPAWI.1714.1]

CASTEEN, ..., in Quebec, 1723. [SPAWI.1723.805]

CATALOGNE, PIERRE, master of La Vierge de la Rochelle from La Rochelle to Newfoundland in 1679. [La Rochelle Archives, Teuleron, 50]

CATOIR, ERNOU, a wool-carder, with his wife and five children, to emigrate to Virginia, 1621. [CSPC.Addenda; Colonial Correspondence, Vol.i,#45]

CELERON,........, a letter to Deputy Governor of Pennsylvania, 1749. [JCTP.1749.45/207]

The French in the Americas, 1620-1820

CERTOMANCHE, ..., Commander of Fort Pontchartrein, Labrador, 1708. [SPAWI.1708.60]

CEURE, JEAN, a French interpreter and officer in Canada, 1730, 1731. [SPAWI.1730.622; 1731.478]

CHABANRS, ISAAC, and son, French refugees, landed in Virginia, 1700. [SPAWI.1700.681]

CHABRAND DE LISLE, DAVID, an Anglican minister in Canada, chaplain to the British garrison at Montreal, 1766. [FPA#325][LIS.5.143]

CHAFFART, ..., in St Kitts, 1673. [SPAWI.1673.1036]

CHAILLAUD, THARE, master of the Catherine de la Rochelle from La Rochelle to Quebec in 1666. [La Rochelle archives]

CHAILLE, BENJAMIN, master of L'Imprevue which was captured when bound from the West Indies in 1744. [NA.HCA32.118/1]

CHAILLE, JEAN, master of the Catherine de la Rochelle from La Rochelle to Quebec in 1667. [La Rochelle archives]

CHAMBEAU, ..., a French soldier captured in Canada, 1759. [SM.21.541]

CHAMBONE, JEDEON, and wife, French refugees, landed in Virginia, 1700. [SPAWI.1700.681]

CHAMPNEYS, JOHN, was granted 800 acres in Granville County, South Carolina, 1738. [NA.CO5.398]

CHAMPLAIN, ..., at Quebec, 1629. [CSPC.V.16]

CHANCY, CHARLES, a laborer, with his wife and two children, to emigrate to Virginia, 1621. [CSPC.Addenda; Colonial Correspondence, Vol.i,#45]

CHAPEAU, MATHIEU, master of La Famille de Nantes which was captured when bound from the West Indies in 1747. [NA.HCA32.112/1]

CHARDONET, ABRAHAM, was granted 300 acres in Granville County, South Carolina, 1738. [NA.CO5.398]

The French in the Americas, 1620-1820

CHARELOYRE, Captain, master of Le Superbe at Martinique, 1702. [SPAWI.1702.195]

CHARLEVOIX, ..., from France as an Inspector of Acadia and Mississippi, 1722. [SPAWI.1722.73]

CHASTAIGNER, ALEXANDER THEZEE, Seigneur de Lisle, land grant in Carolina, 1686. [SPAWI.1686.842]

CHASTAIGNER, HENRY AUGUSTUS, Seigneur de Cramake, land grant in Carolina, 1686. [SPAWI.1686.842]

CHASSALIAN, QUINTIN, a French refugee, landed in Virginia, 1700. [SPAWI.1700.681]

CHASTAINE, ESTIENNE, a French refugee, landed in Virginia, 1700. [SPAWI.1700.681]

CHASTAIN, PIERRE, wife and five children, French refugees, landed in Virginia, 1700. [SPAWI.1700.681]

CHATANIER, PIERRE, wife and brother, French refugees, landed in Virginia, 1700. [SPAWI.1700.681]

CHATEAU RENAUD, Vice Admiral, master of Le Merveilleux at Martinique in 1702. [SPAWI.1702.195]

CHATELIER, RENE, master of La Flore de Nantes which was captured when bound from the West Indies in 1744. [NA.HCA32.112/1]

CHATIN, ..., in Manakin Town, Virginia, 1701. [SPAWI.1701.1176]

CHAVEAU, PIERRE, master of Les Deux Souers de la Rochelle from France to Canada and the West Indies in 1684. [NA.HCA.32.181]

CHAUVET, JEAN, master of the L'Aigle Noir de la Rochelle from La Rochelle to Quebec and the West Indies, 1678. [La Rochelle Municipal Library ms]; master of the St Jean de La Rochelle from Bordeaux to Quebec in 1691. [Charente Maritime Archives, B235, 330-339]

CHAVITEAU, ANDRE, master of L'Havre de Flessingue from La Rochelle to Quebec in 1670; master of Le Neptune de la Rochelle from La Rochelle to Quebec in 1672; master of Diligente de la Rochelle from La Rochelle to Quebec in 1683. [Charente Maritime Archives, B5669/5671.2.184; La Rochelle Archives, Riviere/Teuleron; Gironde Archives. B72/158]

CHAVITEAU, CHARLES, master of La Perle from La Rochelle to Quebec in 1696. [Charente Maritime Archives]

CHEAVIN, ALEXANDER, was granted 150 acres in Craven County, South Carolina, 1738. [NA.CO5.398]

CHEAZIN, ISAAC, was granted 350 acres in Craven County, South Carolina, 1738. [NA.CO5.398]

CHENRS, JEAN, and wife, French refugees, landed in Virginia, 1700. [SPAWI.1700.681]

CHENEZ, CHARLES, master of the sloop Catherine seized at Montserrat, 1736. [SPAWI.1737.61i]

CHEORET, FRANCOIS, master of La Themis which was captured when bound for the West Indies in 1744. [NA.HCA32.154]

CHERPI, GABRIEL, in Grenada, 1769. [JCTP.1769.156]

CHERRIOT, GEORGE, a planter in Nevis, 1712. [JCTP.1712.395]

CHEVALIER, ANTHONY, born 1712, a shoemaker, bound from London to Jamaica s an indentured servant in 1736. [CLRO]

CHEVALIER, JEAN FRANCOIS, of the schooner Romaine de Martinique, at Barbados, 1725. [SPAWI.1725.398]

CHEVALIER, JACQUES, master of the Harman de Tramlade from Newfoundland bound for France in 1673. [APCCol#975]

CHEVALIER, LOUIS, a merchant planter in Antigua, denizised 1665. [SPAWI.1665.376]

The French in the Americas, 1620-1820

CHEVELIS, JOHN, was granted 450 acres in Granville County, South Carolina, 1738. [NA.CO5.398]

CHEVERAUX, Father, a Catholic priest in Cape Sables, Nova Scotia before 1736. [SPAWI.1735.462]

CHEVILETT, JOHN and SARAH, were granted 500 acres in Purryburgh, South Carolina, 1737. [NA.CO5.398]

CHOUPART, DANIEL, was granted 100 acres in Granville County, South Carolina, 1738. [NA.CO5.398]

CHRETIEN, DAVID, master of the Marguerite de Dieppe from La Rochelle to Canada and the West Indies in 1686. [La Rochelle Library, Riviere ms]

CHRISTIANS, DAVID, was granted 250 acres in Granville County, South Carolina, 1738. [NA.CO5.398]

CLERC, FRANCOIS, a French refugee, landed in Virginia, 1700. [SPAWI.1700.681]

CLITDEN, FRANCOIS, a laborer, with his wife and five children, to emigrate to Virginia, 1621. [CSPC.Addenda; Colonial Correspondence, Vol.i,#45]

CLOUET, ELIZABETH, in St Vincent's, 1777. [JCTP.84.69]

COARET, ANTOINE, a French Indian at Les Mines, Nova Scotia, 2 October 1720. [SPAWI.1720.241xiv]

COARET, PIERRE, a French Indian at Les Mines, Nova Scotia, 2 October 1720. [SPAWI.1720.241xiv]

COCHET, ANDRE, a French refugee, landed in Virginia, 1700. [SPAWI.1700.681]

CODROT, CLAUDE, a French inhabitant of Miniss, Nova Scotia, 1720. [SPAWI.1720.180xv]

COIFFIN, JOANNIS, master of Le Chevalier Bart a privateer which was captured when bound from the West Indies in 1744. [NA.HCA32.101/1]

COLLADON, ..., a French minister died in St James', South Carolina, 1733. [FPA#144]

The French in the Americas, 1620-1820

COLLINE, JACQUES, master of Le Marechal de Saxe which was captured when bound from the West Indies in 1747. [NA.HCA32.130/1]

COMBAUD, PIERRE, a Jesuit at La Grande Savanne, St Vincent, 1686. [SPAWI.1686.871xii]

COMBETTE, JACQUES, master of Le Mentor which was captured when bound for the West Indies in 1744. [NA.HCA32.128]

COMPTE, THOMAS, master of the Caiemand which was captured when bound for the West Indies in 1748. [NA.HCA32.103/1]

COMTE, PIERRE, a French refugee, landed in Virginia, 1700. [SPAWI.1700.681]

CONGERIE, ..., master of La Notre Dame de Rosaire de Siboure from La Rochelle via Quebec to the West Indies in 1691. [Charente Maritime Archives, B235]

CONNE, JACQUES, 'a tiller of the earth', with his wife and two children, to emigrate to Virginia, 1621. [CSPC.Addenda; Colonial Correspondence, Vol.i,#45]

CONSEILLERE, ..., a merchant in Charleston, South Carolina, 1724. [SPAWI.1724.85vi]

CONSIDENT, JOHN, a planter in St Kitts, 1712. [JCTP.1712.394]

CONSIDENT, SUSANNAH, in St Kitts, 1712. [JCTP.1712.395]

CONSTANTINE, JEAN, a French refugee, landed in Virginia, 1700. [SPAWI.1700.681]

CORBUSIER, HENRY, a councillor of Bermuda, 1742. [JCTP.1742.31/61]

CORLART, ..., drowned in Lake Champlain when bound for Quebec, 1667. [CSPC.1667.1572]

CORNILLE, PIERRE, a vine dresser, a young man, to emigrate to Virginia, 1621. [CSPC.Addenda; Colonial Correspondence, Vol.i,#45]

CORNU, PIERRE, a French refugee, landed in Virginia, 1700. [SPAWI.1700.681]

The French in the Americas, 1620-1820

CORTEMANCH, ..., commander of the Marines in Labrador, 1704. [SPAWI.1714.2]

COSSART, ..., commander of the French who attacked Montserrat in 1712. [SPAWI.1728.65i]

COSTE, ISAAC, was granted 150 acres in Granville County, South Carolina, 1738. [NA.CO5.398]

COTHONNEAU, ELIAS, brother of William Cothonneau, in New York, both dead by 1715. [SPAWI.1715.297]

COUILLAN DEAU, JEAN, master of <u>Saint Joseph de la Rochelle</u> from La Rochelle and Bordeaux to Quebec in 1692, 1693, 1694; master of <u>Le Comte de Frontenac de la Rochelle</u>, from Bordeaux to Quebec in 1699. [Charente Maritime Archives, B235/B5687-8; Gironde Archives#6B298; La Rochelle Archives, Grenot; Bordeaux Archives, Lalanne]

COULET,......, a French minister in South Carolina, died in 1732. [FPA#143/144]

COUPET, FRANCOIS, a French refugee, landed in Virginia, 1700. [SPAWI.1700.681]

COURPOM, ..., a planter in St Kitts before 1717. [JCTP.1717.260]

COUSIER, ..., commander of a squadron from Toulouse to the Caribbean, 1712. [SPAWI.1712.33ii]

COUSSEAU, JAMES, a free denizen of New York, 1669. [SPAWI.1669.29]

COUTURIER, Sieur, in South Carolina, 1724. [JCTP.1724.84/108/110]

CREVIER, ..., a prisoner brought from Canada to Albany, New York, in 1693. [SPAWI.1693.612iii]

CROISET, ..., a land grant in Carolina by the King of France, 1715. [JCTP.1715.57]

CROISSEL, ..., a French officer in Quebec, 1723. [SPAWI.1723.805]

CROIZET, ..., a French officer in Acadia, 1721. [SPAWI.1721.743]

The French in the Americas, 1620-1820

CUPPER, PIERRE, a French refugee, landed in Virginia, 1700. [SPAWI.1700.681]

D'ABBADIE, ..., Governor of Louisiana, 1763. [HLF]

DAGUENET, JEAN FRANCOIS, master of Providence de Grandville which was captured bound from Newfoundland to France in 1746. [NA.HCA32.147/1]

D'AIGNAN, JEAN PIERRE, master of L'Hercule which was captured when bound from Cayenne in 1746. [NA.HCA32.117]

DAINE, FRANCOIS, at Lake Champlain, Quebec, 1763. [JCTP.1763.309]

DALBAIE, DAVID, was granted 200 acres in Craven County, South Carolina, 1738. [NA.CO5.398]

D'AMBLEMONT, Marquis, in St Kitts, 1697, 1698. [SPAWI.1697.639/715/859/978; 1698.1089]

DAMONT, JAN, a Walloon laborer, with his wife, to emigrate to Virginia, 1621. [CSPC.Addenda; Colonial Correspondence, Vol.i,#45]

D'ANGEAC, FRANCOIS GABRIEL, Governor of St Pierre and Miquelon, 1763 to 1773.

DANGLA, ESTIENNE, master of Le Chasseur which was captured when bound from the West Indies in 1747. [NA.HCA32.102/2]

DANIELL, ..., master of the ...... from Dieppe to Cape Breton, 1629/1630. [CSPC.V.80]

DANJEAC, ..., Governor of St Pierre and Miquelon, 1764. [JCTP.1764.119/469]

DARDAGUIETTE, DIRON, Governor of Mobile, 1735. [SPAWI.1735.157]

D'ARGUIBELL, Captain PHILIBERT, in Acadia, 1722. [SPAWI.1722.234viiic]

DARLING, ..., Chevalier de St Louis, a French soldier captured in Canada, 1759. [SM.21.541]

DARRACHE, JEAN, master of La Catherine which was captured when bound for the West Indies in 1745-1746. [NA.HCA32.102/1]

The French in the Americas, 1620-1820

D'ARRIGRAND, Sieur GRATIAN, claim for land in Cape Breton, 1764; granted 20,000 acres there in July 1764. [JCTP.1764.218][APCCol.1764.app.v]

DARTIQUE,......, a French soldier captured in Canada, 1759. [SM.21.541]

DARTIS, JACQUES, master of the privateer Le Roland which was captured when bound for the West Indies in 1747. [NA.HCA32.150]

DASSIE, MARTIN, master of La Gracieuse which was captured when bound for Quebec in 1745. [NA.HCA32.113/1]

DAUBERMINY, JOHN PETER, in Dominica, 1771. [JCTP.1773.274]

D'AULNEY, Sieur, Governor of Acadia, 1667. [SPAWI.1667.1644]

D'AUTEVIL, ..., a French officer in Boston, New England, 1714. [SPAWI.1715.568iii]

D'AVAUX, ..., the French king's lieutenant on Marie Galante, 1691. [SPAWI.1691.1557]

DAVID, ELIZABETH, in St Vincent, dead by 1772. [JCTP.1772.319]

D'BOURNE, ..., near the Quebec River, 1711. [JCTP.1711.673]

DE AMBLIMONT, Marquis, Governor of Martinique, 1698; Governor of the French Islands in America, 1701. [SPAWI.1698.1054/1089; 1701.224]

DE ASSAS, Viscompte, Major du Place, St Domingo, 1796. [NRS.GD188.28.6]

D'EAU, Chevalier, a prisoner in New York, 1688, 1691. [SPAWI.1691.955/957/1398/2220.2515i; 1696.262]

DEAUTELL, ..., at St Francis, Quebec, 1721. [SPAWI.1723.805]

DEAUVILLES, JOHN, died in Jamaica, probate 1696, Prerogative Court of Canterbury.

DE BAAS, ..., French Lieutenant General in America, 1669; Governor of Martinique, 1672. [SPAWI.1669.52; 1672.901]

DE BAT, THEOPHILUS, was granted 5000 acres in West Florida, 1765. [APCCol.1765.App.V]

The French in the Americas, 1620-1820

DE BAT, JOSEPH, was granted 5000 acres in West Florida, 1765. [APCCol.1765.App.V]

DE BEAUCHAMP,........, an army officer with 25 years service in Louisiana by 1759. [Archive des Colonies, serie D, troupes colonials, registres D 2C.50/58]

DE BEAUCHAMP, BOURKE, in Dominica, 1771. [JCTP.1773.274]

DE BEAUFAIN, HECTOR BERENGER, was granted lot 153 in Purryburgh, and 800 acres in Granville County, South Carolina, 1738. [NA.CO5.398]; a Councillor of South Carolina, 1747; probate 1767, Prerogative Court of Canterbury. [APCCol.1747.app.II][JCTP.1747.226/261]

DE BEAUHARNAIS, Marquis CHARLES, Governor of Canada, 1730; letters, 1737. [SPAWI.1730.622; 1737.211/212]

DE BELLEORME, JACQUES SIMON, Governor of St Pierre and Miquelon, 1694 to 1702.

DE BENOIST,........, Commandant of Fort Des Alibamons, 1736; an army officer with 23 years service in Louisiana by 1759. [Archive des Colonies, serie D, troupes colonials, registres D 2C.50/58]

DE BERNIERE, CHARLES, was granted land in New York for a settlement of French Protestants, 1765. [APCCol.1765.819]

DE BERNIERE, JOHN, was granted land in New York for a settlement of French Protestants, 1765. [APCCol.1765.819]

DE BERVILLE, Sieur, born in Canada, Governor of St Louis, 1708. [SPAWI.1708.60]

DE BLAQUIERE, HENRY, son of Peter Boyle De Blaquiere, married Lucretia Light, 4th daughter of Colonel Light late of the 25th Regiment, in Lytis, Carey, Woodstock, Upper Canada, on 11 October 1848. [GM.NS31.198]

DE BLAINVILLE, CELERON, Commandant at Detroit, 1749. [HLF]

DE BLANC,........, born 1679, an army officer with 41 years service in Louisiana by 1759. [Archive des Colonies, serie D, troupes colonials, registres D 2C.50/58]

The French in the Americas, 1620-1820

DE BLENAC, le Comte, Governor of Martinique, 1678, 1679, ; Chief Governor of the French Islands, 1699; captured St Kitts. [SPAWI.1678.741ix; 1679.871; 1682.654; 1689.3/355/etc/ 1699.649; 1707.467]

DE BLOIS, LEWIS, late merchant in Boston, New England, died in Holburn on 9 February 1799. [GM.69.173]

DE BOAKE, JOSEPH, a prisoner at Fort Orange, Albany, New York, 1696. [SPAWI.1696.370ii]

DE BOMPAR, Marquis, Governor of Martinique, letters, 1750. [JCTP.1750, 1751.151/185]

DE BONAVENTURE, PIERRE DENYS, master of St Jean de la Rochelle, from France to Canada in 1689, [La Rochelle Archives, Riviers and Soullard #14]; master of the L'Armes de la Compagnie de la Rochelle, from La Rochelle to Canada in 1690. [Charente Maritime Archives]; master of Le Profond from France to Quebec, Acadia and Newfoundland in 1696. [French Colonial Archives: ACClId.3/170]

DE BONAVENTURE, ..., in Acadia, 1698. [SPAWI.1698.922i/988xi]

DE BONILLE,........, an army officer with 31 years service in Louisiana by 1759. [Archive des Colonies, serie D, troupes colonials, registres D 2C.50/58]

DE BONNEMERE, DANIEL, a Huguenot and planter of Bonnemere's Plantation, Pentecoste Division, St Kitts, later in Jamaica, before 1715. [APCCol.1715.1225] [SPAWI.1714.630vii/ix; 1715.375/431]

DE BONNEMERE, PAUL MINVIELLE, a Huguenot, son of Daniel de Bonnemere in St Kitts, estates restored in 1715. [APCCol.1715.1225] [SPAWI.1714.630vii; 1715.375]

DE BOURBON, L. A., Conseil de Marine to the Lieutenant General and Intendant of the French Windward Islands, 1720. [SPAWI.1729.1053]

DE BOURE, LOUIS, master of the Postillion a pirate vessel in the West Indies, 1716. [SPAWI.1716.425iii]

The French in the Americas, 1620-1820

DE BOURGMONT, ETIENNE VENIARD, Commandant of the Mississippi, 1719. [HLF]

DE BOURVILLE,........., Commander in Chief of an expedition to Hudson Bay, 1694. [SPAWI.1696.471]

DE BOYNEAU, ..., commander of two French men o'war in the Caribbean, 1672. [SPAWI.1672.901]

DE BRETTON, Baroness JUDITH, eldest daughter of Baron Frederick de Bretton in St Croix, married Lieutenant Cumming, in Guadaloupe in 1812. [GM.81.188]

DE BREUIL, ROSE, a widow in Dominica, 1771. [JCTP.1773.248]

DE BRESLAI, ..., in Nova Scotia, 1732. [SPAWI.1732.259]

DE BRISAC, Captain, in St Kitts, 1717. [JCTP.1717.261]

DE BRISSAQ, PAUL, a planter on Nevis, 1712. [JCTP]

DE BRISSON, ANNE ST., in St Kitts, 1712. [JCTP.1712.395]

DE BROSSES, ELIAS, owner of the Maxwell which captured the French snow Bon Rencontre 250 tons, on 22 March 1757. [APCCol.1765.591]

DE BROUILLAN, SAINT OVIDE, arrived at Port Royal, Acadia, 1701; Governor of Port Royal, 1704; the French King's Lieutenant at Placentia, 1709; Governor of Cape Breton, Governor of Canada; 1719; 1720; 1727; 1728; 1732; 1733;1736. [SPAWI.1701.785/820/933/952/978; 1704.260/1017; 1709.890; 1717.213; 1720.241; 1727.789; 1728.395; 1732.454; 1733.439; 1736.462][JCTP. 1728.413]

DE BRUTER, JOHN, and his sons John and William, in Baltimore County, Maryland, naturalised, 1701. [SPAWI.1701.447][NA.CO5.744.74/92]

D'BUKE, ..., French coastguard in the West Indies, 1723. [SPAWI.1723.496ii]

DE CAEN, EMORY, master of Bon Dieu at Quebec, trading with the Huron for furs, 1629, 1631. [CSPC.VI.23]

The French in the Americas, 1620-1820

DE CAEN, WILLIAM, Lord of La Motte, General of the Fleet of New France, 1630. [CSPC.V.87ii]; master of Lyon de Dieppe from Quebec to France in 1633. [SPAWI.1633.75]

DE CALLIERES, Chevalier HECTOR, Governor of Canada, 1698, 1699. [SPAWI.1698.622; 1699.494iii, 675, 771, 1011]

DE CARPENTIER, MARTIN, a brass founder, a young man, to emigrate to Virginia, 1621. [CSPC.Addenda; Colonial Correspondence, Vol.i,#45]

DE CARPENTRY, JAN, a Walloon laborer, with his wife and two children, to emigrate to Virginia, 1621. [CSPC.Addenda; Colonial Correspondence, Vol.i,#45]

DE CARTERET, CHARLES, co-owner of the Two Friends a brig which was condemned by the Vice Admiralty of Quebec on 17 October 1764 on a charge of smuggling wine. [APCCol.1765.610]

DE CARVILLE, Cadet of Marines, Captain of the Guienne Regiment, a French soldier captured in Canada, 1759. [SM.21.541]

DE CAS, ..., Governor of Petit Guavas, 1701. [SPAWI.1701.814]

DE CASSE, Admiral, in the West Indies, 1691. [SPAWI.1691.1546

DE CASSEAUX, FRANCOISE MARIE JEANNE GODDARD, in Dominica, 1773. [JCTP.1773.334]

DE CASTES, ..., of Languedoc, a French soldier captured in Canada, 1759. [SM.21.541]

DE CAYLUS, Marquis, Governor of Martinique, 1749. [JCTP.1749.398/450]

DE CHAMBRE, ..., in St Kitts, 1672; 1701. [SPAWI.1672.903; 1701.1091/1130/1133]

DE CHAMOIS, JEAN BAPTISTE DU PLESSIS, in St Vincent, 1772. [JCTP.1772.319]

DE CHAMP, FRANCIS, was granted 291 acres in Berlkey County, South Carolina, 1737. [NA.CO5.398]

The French in the Americas, 1620-1820

DE CHAMPIGNY, Marquis, Governor of the French West Indies, in Guadaloupe or Martinique, 1722, 1723, 1730, 1731, 1736/1737, 1740. [SPAWI.1722.419; 1723.486; 1730. 110; 1731.256; 1736.296; 1737.61/318][JCTP.1731.236; 1740.333]

DE CHANTELOUP, FAVRY, at the Baye de Phillipeaux, Labrador, 1764. [JCTP.1764.219]

DE CHAROY,........, an army officer with 19 years service in Louisiana by 1759. [Archive des Colonies, serie D, troupes colonials, registres D 2C.50/58]

DE CHATEAU REGNANT, Le Chevalier, master of Le Orgeleux at Martinique in 1702. [SPAWI.1702.195]

DE CHATEAU RENAULT,............., naval commander in the West Indies, 1701. [SPAWI.1701.516]

DE CHEVRY, ..., settled at Louisbourg, Cape Breton, before 1756, a merchant there trading with Quebec, captured by the British in the St Lawrence in 1758 and employed by them as a pilot, died soon after leaving a wife and four children, a petition by his widow in 1771. [CalHOP.1771/715]

DE CLARETT, ..., in St Kitts, 1672. [SPAWI.1672.903]

DE CLARKE, DANIEL, in New York, 1689. [SPAWI.1689.352/459]

DE CLERMONT DIEL, ..., Governor of Martinique, 1663. [CSPC.1663.578/581/617]

DE COASTEBELL, ..., commander at Placentia, Newfoundland, 1699. [SPAWI.1699.793]

DE COATLEGON,........, naval commander in the West Indies, 1701. [SPAWI.1701.516]

DE COMBES, JANNER, master of L'Armes de Zelande from La Rochelle to Newfoundland and Quebec in 1662. [La Rochelle Municipal Library]

DE CONDRAY, Captain, master of Le Henry at Martinique in 1702. [SPAWI.1702.195]

The French in the Americas, 1620-1820

DE CONTRECOEUR, ..., at Fort Duquesnes, Ohio, 1754. [HLF]

DE COSTEBELLE, LOUIS DE PASTEUR, born 1658, Captain of St Pierre and Miquelon in 1689; Governor of Newfoundland, 1702, at Placentia, 6 May 1709; at Placentia, 22 July 1714, died 1732. [SPAWI.1704.315d; 1709.890iv; 1715.194x/658]

DE COSTY, JEAN, in Antigua, 1709. [SPAWI.1709.487ii]

DE COULER, Captain, killed by the Chicachas at Fort Saint Claude in 1730. [HLF]

DE COURCELLE, ..., Governor General of Canada, 1666. [CSPC.1666.1228]

DE COURCERAC, Lieutenant, at Martinique, 1751. [JCTP.1751.185]

DE COWETT, ..., in St Kitts, 1672. [SPAWI.1672.903]

DE CRENNE, JAN DE, a Walloon, a 'fritteur' – a glass-maker (?), with his wife and child, to emigrate to Virginia, 1621. [CSPC.Addenda; Colonial Correspondence, Vol.i,#45]

DE CREPY, ABEL, a Walloon shuttle worker, with his wife and four children, to emigrate to Virginia, 1621. [CSPC.Addenda; Colonial Correspondence, Vol.i,#45]

DE CRISAFI, Marquis, an Italian, Governor of Trois Rivieres, Quebec, 1708. [SPAWI.1708.60]

DE CROY, JAN, a Walloon sawyer, with his wife and five children, to emigrate to Virginia, 1621. [CSPC.Addenda; Colonial Correspondence, Vol.i,#45]

DE CUSSY, ..., Governor of Petit Guavos, 1684; Governor of St Domingo, 1689. [SPAWI.1684.1759/1839; 1689.52/2782]

DE DENONVILLE, Marquis, Governor of Canada, 1687, a land grant, 1689; 1698. [SPAWI.1687.1160; 1698.622ix; 1732.259]

DE DORGON,........, an army officer with 21 years service in Louisiana by 1759. [Archive des Colonies, serie D, troupes colonials, registres D 2C.50/58]

DE EMILION, GABRIEL, and his son Charles, servants, from Virginia to Maryland, 1701. [SPAWI.1701.1168]

The French in the Americas, 1620-1820

D'ENTREMONT, CHARLES, residing on the Pomoncoops River, Nova Scotia, 1732. [SPAWI.1732.259]

D'EON, ..., in Grenada, 1763. [JCTP.1763.386]

D'ESNOS, ..., in Martinique, 1704. [SPAWI.1705.1025i]

D'ESTAING, le Comte, Governor of St Domingo, 1763. [Cal.H.O.pp.1764/1459]

D'ESTREES, le Comte, French General or Admiral in the Caribbean, 1677. [SPAWI.1677.48; 1678.603]

DE FEUIL, PIERRE, master of the Phoenix of Nantes fishing on the Banks of Newfoundland, 1723. [SPAWI.1723.739ii]

DE FIELD, JAMES, in the Caribee Islands, dead by 1677. [SPAWI.1677.415]

DE FLECHIE, Chevalier, Major du Place, St Domingo, 1796. [NRS.GD188.28.6]

DE FORREST, JESSE, petitioned the Privy Council to permit the settlement of 60 families of Walloons and French Protestants, to settle in Virginia, July 1621, [SPAWI.1621.114]; a dyer, with his wife and five children, to emigrate to Virginia, 1621. [CSPC.Addenda; Colonial Correspondence, Vol.i,#45]

DE FRANQUESNAY, ..., in St Domingo, 1690. [SPAWI.1690.2782]

DE FRONTENAC, Count, Governor of Canada, dead by 1699. [SPAWI.1698.622; 1699.130/250/266/1011xxv]

DE GENILLAT, JEAN FRANCOIS, Swiss, land grant in Carolina, 1685. [SPAWI.1685.295]

DE GENISNE MOUNIER, Captain, master of Le Saint Louis at Martinique in 1702. [SPAWI.1702.195]

DE GENNES, ..., a French officer who was court martialed in Martinique, 1704. [SPAWI.1705.1025i]

DE GIGNILLAT, JAMES, a missionary in Goose Creek, South Carolina, possibly returned to Europe in 1713. [FPA#130/131]

DE GOURDE, Captain, commander of Fort ......, Quebec, 1711. [JCTP.1711.673]

The French in the Americas, 1620-1820

DE GRAEFS, PETER, in St Kitts, a deposition, 1682. [SPAWI.1682.602xviii]

DE GRANCEY, Marquis, French naval commander at Martinique, 1675. [SPAWI.1675.706]

DE GRAND, FRANCIS, pastor of a French church in St Kitts, 1727. [FPA#276]

DE GRANDPRE, Captain, master of Le Prudent at Martinique in 1702. [SPAWI.1702.195]

DE GRANDPRES, ..., an army officer with 27 years service in Louisiana by 1759. [Archive des Colonies, serie D, troupes colonials, registres D 2C.50/58]

DE GRAVE, ..., Captain of Rousillon, a French soldier captured in Canada, 1759. [SM.21.541]

DE GRUCHY, PHILIP, petitioned for land in Nova Scotia, 1767. [JCTP.74.182]

DE GUERCHY, Count, in 1765, petitioned regarding his lands in Labrador which had been seized at the taking of Isle Vederonne and Niganiche at the entry to Baye Royale. [JCTP.72.381]

DE GUITANDE, ..., Governor of Martinique, 1701. [SPAWI.1701.1192]

DE HABILENE, PHILISIBERT, captain of a French ship that attacked the Canso settlement in Nova Scotia, 1720. [SPAWI.1720.241ii]

DE HAMELL, ..., in St Kitts, 1672. [SPAWI.1672.903]

DE HARISMENDY, LOUIS, master of La Glorieux de Bordeaux from France to Quebec and Newfoundland in 1690. [Gironde Archives]

D'HINSE, ..., a surgeon at Orange, Canada, 1666. [CSPC.1666.1226/7/9]

DE HIRIBERRY, JOANNIS, a merchant of St John de Luz, at the Island of Canso, Canada, 1718, 1719. [SPAWI.1719.208iv][APCCol.1721.1314]

DE HIROYEN, PASCATO, master of Saint Pierre de Bayonne , from La Rochelle to Newfoundland, St Pierre, and Quebec in 1679. [La Rochelle Archives, Teuleron]

The French in the Americas, 1620-1820

D'IBERVILLE, ..., commander of the French men o'war Pollisht and the Salamander in Hudson Bay, 1716. [JCTP.1719.95]

DE JOURDENEAU, Captain M., a French soldier captured in Canada, 1759. [SM.21.541]

DE JOUX, ..., French minister at Manakin Town, King William parish, Virginia, 1701. [SPAWI.1701.719]

DE JUMONVILLE, Le Chevalier COULON, an officer in Ohio, 1754. [HLF]

DE KERLEREC, ..., in New Orleans, letters, 1756/1757. [JCTP.1757.341]

DE LA BARRE, ..., Governor of Martinique, 1669. [SPAWI.1668.1669.19/39/56/etc]

DE LA BARRE, LE FEBURE, 1683; at Camp de la Chine, Canada, 1684. [SPAWI.1683.1863.1; 1684.1817i]

DE LA BOURLARDIE, Sieur, claim to land in Cape Breton, 1765. [JCTP.1765.237/239]

DE LA BUTTE FRERORT, GUILLAUME, Captain of L'Henriette a privateer which captured when bound for the West Indies in 1745. [NA.HCA32.117]

DE LA CHASSE, Father PIERRE, a missionary at Penobscot, Acadia, 1715; in Quebec, 1722. [SPAWI.1715.142iii; 1722.73ii]

DE LA CHESNAYE, Sieur, in Quebec, 1691. [SPAWI.1691.1430]

DE LA CLOCHE, JOHN, in New Jersey, 1693. [SPAWI.1693.1313]

DE LA COMBIERE, Captain of Marines, Chevalier de St Louis, a French soldier captured in Canada, 1759. [SM.21.541]

DE LA CONSEILLERE, BENJAMIN, in Charleston, South Carolina, 1715, 1716, 1728. [SPAWI.1715.642iii; 1716.407I; 1729.807ii]

DE LA CONTRY, N., master of La Charmante which was captured when bound from the West Indies in 1745. [NA.HCA32.160/2]

The French in the Americas, 1620-1820

DE LA COUSAYE, ALETTA, daughter of the late Captain Van Del Bourgh a planter and a Huguenot in St Kitts, before 1715, who fled to the English sector to avoid persecution; estates restored in 1715. [APCCol.1715.1225][SPAWI.1714.639iv; 1715.375]

DE LA CROIX, JOHN, pilot of the Count de Paix, bound from St Domingo for Havre de Grace, France, in September 1713, was grounded near the island of Henegua. [SPAWI.1716.247i]; in Bermuda and Virginia, 1716. [JCTP.1716.170]

DE LA DICQ, LAWRENCE, citizen and joiner of London, died aboard the ship Bevor bound for New York, probate 1691, Prerogative Court of Canterbury.

DE LA FENELON, ..., in Martinique, 1763. [JCTP.1763.384]

DE LA FERTE, ABRAHAM PICARD, in Antigua, 1730. [APCCol.1730.177]

DE LA FONTAINE, Sieur, claimed the Mingan Islands on the coast of Labrador, 1763. [JCTP.1763.382]

DE LA FOREST, Father CHARLES, in Martinique, 1689. [SPAWI.1689.157iv]

DE LA FOREST, GABRIEL, a servant of the Canada Company of France, 1696, 1697. [SPAWI.1696.1350; 1697.473/500/541/591/603/761]

DE LA FOREST, ..., Governor of York alias Bourbon Fort, Hudson Bay, 1696, 1697, 1716. [SPAWI.1696.1345; 1697.584; 1698.398/449][JCTP.1719.95]

DE LA FREILLE, ..., a French Protestant in St Kitts, 1716. [JCTP.1716.197]

DE LA GAL, JOHN, in South Carolina administration, 1769, Prerogative Court of Canterbury.

DE LA GOUDALIE, Pere CHARLES, at Minis, Cobaquit, Nova Scotia, 1732. [SPAWI.1732.259/455]

DE LA HARPE, JEAN BAPTISTE BENARD, born in St Malo in 1683, to Louisiana in 1718 with 40 settlers. [HLF]

DE LA HERE, HENRY, was granted lot 118 in Purrysburgh, Granville County, South Carolina, 1738. [NA.CO5.398]

The French in the Americas, 1620-1820

DE LA JONQUIERE, ..., Governor of Canada, 1749, 1751; in Nova Scotia, 1752. [JCTP.1749.2; 1751.258; 1752.303]

DE LALY, MATURIN, master of Le Duc de Villeroy which was captured when bound from the West Indies in 1747. [NA.HCA32.105]

DE LA MAINE, WROTH, in Jamaica, died around 1683. [APCCol.1708.1065]

DE LA MAIRE, JOHN, in Maryland, 1674. [SPAWI.1674.1310]

DE LA MARLIER, NICOLAS, a dyer, with his wife and two children, to emigrate to Virginia, 1621. [CSPC.Addenda; Colonial Correspondence, Vol.i,#45]

DE LAMBERVILLE, JACQUES, a Jesuit in Canada, 1686. [SPAWI.1686.969]

DE LA LUZERNE, Chevalier, a French officer in America, letters, 1783. [HMC.IV.16/23/236]

DE LA MET, JAN, a Walloon young man, a laborer, to emigrate to Virginia, 1621. [CSPC.Addenda; Colonial Correspondence, Vol.i,#45]

DE LA MONTAGNE, ..., a medical student, 'a marrying man', to emigrate to Virginia, 1621. [CSPC.Addenda; Colonial Correspondence, Vol.i,#45]

DE LA MONTAGNE, ..., an apothecary and surgeon, 'a marrying man', to emigrate to Virginia, 1621. [CSPC.Addenda; Colonial Correspondence, Vol.i,#45]

DE LA MOTHE-CADILLAC, ..., Governor of Louisiana, 1710. [HLF]

DE LA MOTTE, FRANCOIS, master of Le Charles Auguste a privateer which was captured when bound from the West Indies in 1747. [NA.HCA32.103/1]

DE LA MUCE, Marquis OLIVIER, settled in Norfolk County, Virginia, 1700; part owner of the Mary Ann 1701. [FPA#161][SPAWI.1701.228/1042liii]

DE LANY, CAVAN, born in Paris during 1709, a clerk, bound from London to Maryland as an indentured servant in 1731. [CLRO]

DE LA PAGERIE, Madame, mother of Madame Bonaparte, died in Martinique on 1 July 1807 and was buried on Les Trois Islets. [GM.77.888]

The French in the Americas, 1620-1820

DE LA PLACE, HENRY, a French Protestant, petitioned to be shipped to America, possibly went to Jamaica, 1682. [SPAWI.1682.883]

DE LA PIVARDIERE, JOSEPH RICHARD, master of La Marie Francoise which was captured when bound for the West Indies in 1744. [NAHCA32.130/1]

DE LA POITERIE, Le Chevalier, in Nevis, 1674. [SPAWI.1674.1333]

DE LA RADE, ..., master of ......of Dieppe, off Ferryland, Newfoundland, 1628. [CSPC.Vol.IV]

DE LA RIVIERE, ..., in Martinique, 1763. [JCTP.1763.384]

DE L'ARNAGE, ..., Lieutenant Governor of Hispaniola, 1738. [SPAWI.1738.417/447]

DE LA ROIZE, Captain, master of Le Capable at Martinique in 1702. [SPAWI.1702.195]

DE LA RONDE, Captain DENYS, at Annapolis Royal 1715; an officer at Cape Breton, 1733. [SPAWI.1715.159/287/etc; 1733.440]

DE LA ROUZE, Dr, a planter in Barbados, 1699. [SPAWI.1699.732]

DE LA SOMET, JOHN, born 1636, died in Virginia during 1766. [GM.36.599]

DE LA SONDON, ..., an army officer, killed by the Chicachas at Fort Saint Claude in 1730. [HLF]

DE LA TOUR, CLAUDE, Commander of the French at Port Royal, 1630. [CSPC.V.102i][SPAWI.1699.108; 1709.554;1733.367]

DE LA TOUR, ..., was granted land and a seigneury in Acadia in 1703. [SPAWI.1730.563]

DE LA TOUR, JAMES SAINT ETIENNE, and his children James, Charles, Ann, Margaret, and Ann, at Menis on the Bay of Fundy, before 1732. [SPAWI.1732.259]

DE LA VALETTE, Chevalier, a French officer in Philadelphia, letters, 1783. [HMC.IV.27/36]

The French in the Americas, 1620-1820

DE LAVALL, THOMAS, in New York, probate, 1683, Prerogative Court of Canterbury.

DE LA VERENDRYE, PIERRE GAULTHIER DE VARENNES, born 1685, an explorer of the West, died 1749. [HLF]

DE LAVILLAR, Captain, master of Le Biguare at Martinique in 1702. [SPAWI.1702.195]

DE LAURENS, ..., in St Kitts, 1689. [SPAWI.1689.193]

DE LA WAFER, LIONEL, a pirate in Virginia, 1689. [APCCol.1689.279]

DELAS, JAMES, was granted 300 acres in Granville County, South Carolina, 1737. [NA.CO5.398]

DE LECHEILLES, JACQUES, a brewer, 'a marrying man', to emigrate to Virginia, 1621. [CSPC.Addenda; Colonial Correspondence, Vol.i,#45]

DE LE GALL, ..., a wheelwright in Georgia, 1738. [SPAWI.1738.157]

DE LE GOLLISSOMIERE, Captain, master of L'Esperance at Martinique in 1702. [SPAWI.1702.195]

DE LE MER, PHILIPPE, a carpenter, a young man, to emigrate to Virginia, 1621. [CSPC.Addenda; Colonial Correspondence, Vol.i,#45]

DE LENO, ..., a member of the Council of Quebec, 1711. [JCTP.1711.673]

DE LE SCURE, DAVID, was granted 150 acres in Granville County, South Carolina, 1738. [NA.CO5.398]

DE LESTER, alias BEAUJOUR, PIERRE, a former house builder in Quebec, witness to a Loyalist claim, 1786. [NA.13.24.136-143]

DE LESEY, Chevalier, Governor of Cayanne, 1676. [SPAWI.1676.918]

DE LESTRE, PIERRE, a house builder in Quebec, 1776, witness to a Loyalist claim of 1786. [NA.AO13.24.136-143]

DE LEUZE, Captain, in St Kitts, 1718. [JCTP.1718.369]

The French in the Americas, 1620-1820

DE LICQUES, PETER, Sieur des Antheux of Picardy, promoted settlement in Carolina in 1630, also in the West Indies and Virginia in 1634; was appointed Receiver General of Revenue from America, in 1632. [CSPCol.vol.VI.42/52; vol.VIII.19]

DE LIELATE, ANTHOINE, a vine dresser, with his wife and four children, to emigrate to Virginia, 1621. [CSPC.Addenda; Colonial Correspondence, Vol.i,#45]

DE LIGREE, Captain, master of L'Assiere at Martinique, 1702. [SPAWI.1702.195]

DE LILLY, JAMES, servant to the Governor of St Kitts in 1654. [CSPCol.1654.XII]

DE LION, ... in Basseterre, Guadaloupe, 1672. [SPAWI.1672.987]

DE LISLE, CHABIAN, an Anglican chaplain in Montreal, 1769. [FPA#9]

DE LISLE, Reverend DAVID CHABRAND, was granted 5,000 acres in Canada, 1766. [APCCol.1766.App.V]

DE LOMBARDS, Sieur, from France to Canada, 1630. [CSPC.V]

DE LOME, PIERRE, and his wife, French refugees, landed in Virginia, 1700. [SPAWI.1700.681]

DE LOMESIL, ..., to Canada, 1689. [SPAWI.1689.348]

DE LOMPRE DU CHEMIN, DANIEL, a Huguenot planter in St Kitts, fled to the English sector to avoid persecution, pre 1714. [SPAWI.1714.630xiii/xv]

DE LONGUEIL, ..., Commandant in Canada, 1726. 361/362; 1727.684]

DE LONGUEIL, ..., a Councillor of Quebec, 1777. [JCTP.Vol.84.106]

DE LONGUILLEE, ..., an interpreter from Canada at Onnondage, New York, 1709. [JCTP.1711.834i]

DE LORME, FRANCOIS, master of La Catherine de Nantes captured when bound from the West Indies in 1744; master of La Mutine which was captured when bound for the West Indies in 1748. [NA.HCA32.103/1; 129]

The French in the Americas, 1620-1820

DE LORME, PIERRE, French refugee, landed in Virginia, 1700. [SPAWI.1700.681]

DE LOVINER, ..., Lieutenant and Aide-Major of the French forces in Canada, pre 1689. [SPAWI.1689.1]

DE LEUZE, Captain JAMES, husband of the only surviving child of Edmund Helot who died in St Kitts in 1680. [SPAWI.1718.510]

DE LYON, ABRAHAM, a wine cultivator in Savannah, Georgia, 1738. [SPAWI.1738.143]

DE LYON, JULIEN, alleged to have looted a factory at Cape Lopez in the West Indies, 1726. [SPAWI.1726.205]

DE LYON, ..., Governor of Guadaloupe, 1668. [CSPC.1668.1740]

DE MACCARTY,........, an army officer with 32 years service in Louisiana by 1763. [Archive des Colonies, serie D, troupes colonials, registres D 2C.50/58]

DE MALHERBE, ..., a French artillery officer at Fort Royal, Martinique, sent to combat pirates, 21 February 1721. [SPAWI.1721.501vii/xiii]

DE MANGLE, Captain, master of a French privateer in the West Indies, 1672. [SPAWI.1672.785]

DE MACHAULT, ..., Intendant of the French Islands in America, 1705. [SPAWI.1705.860i]

DE MARE, JOHN, near the Quebec River, 1711. [JCTP.1711.673]

DE MAREST, JEAN, a revolutionary leader in New York, 1689. [SPAWI.1689.217]

DE MARSALL, LOUIS, a planter on St Kitts, 1712. [JCTP]

DE MARISSER, ...,of de Languedoc, a French soldier captured in Canada, 1759. [SM.21.541]

DE MARTEL, JACQUES ADAM, chaplain to the French Protestants at Cap de Sable, Nova Scotia, 1767. [FPA#7]

The French in the Americas, 1620-1820

DE MAY, ... at Lake Champlain, New York, 1769. [JCTP.1769.69]

DE MERIE, Captain RAYMOND, in South Carolina, 1750, 1757. [JCTP.1750.64; 1757.306]

DE MERVEILLEUX, ..., Captain of a company of Swiss soldiers in the service of the French Mississippi Company, which mutinied at sea and landed at Charleston, South Carolina, 1722. [SPAWI.1722.372vi]

DE MERVELE, GABRIEL, born in Bordeaux, settled in New York in 1666. [NA. Rex-v.The Batchelor, 1674]

DE MESOILE, PHILIP, a pirate, 1689. [SPAWI.1689.85ii]

DE METRES, JOHN, born 1698, died at Montego Bay, Jamaica, in November 1801. [GM.72.181]

DE MIMIE, ..., in St Kitts, 1672. [SPAWI.1672.903]

DE MONGRON, Captain, master of L'Surrene at Martinique, 1702. [SPAWI.1702.195]

DE MONS, ..., of the County of Lacadie in France, was granted lands in Canada by Henry IV of France on 8 November 1603. [JCTP.1750.58]

DE MONSEGAR, MICHEL, at Placentia, Newfoundland, 1694, 1696. [SPAWI.1710.506]

DE MONTIGNY, Chevalier, from France to Canada, 1630. [CSPC.V]

DE MONTCLAIR, Chevalier, from France to Canada, 1630. [CSPC.V]

DE MONTMOLLIN, DAVID FRANCIS, an Anglican minister in Canada, 1768, in Quebec, 1770. [FPA#325][LIS.5.143]

DE MOUCHET, ..., in St Kitts, 1673. [SPAWI.1674.1273]

DE MUY, ..., Governor of Louisiana, 1707. [HLF]

D'ENAMBUE, ..., settled St Kitts or St Lucia, 1626. [SPAWI.1730.324]

The French in the Americas, 1620-1820

DE NAMPONE, MARGARET, a Huguenot and a planter at Cabesterre, St Kitts, around 1695, 1714, estates restored in 1715. [APCCol.1715.1225][SPAWI.1714.630x; 1715.375]

DE NAMPONE, MARY, a Huguenot and a planter at Cabesterre, St Kitts, around 1695, 1714, estates restored in 1715. [APCCol.1715.1225][SPAWI.1714.630x; 1715.375]

DE NAMPONE, Dr, a planter in St Kitts before 1714. [SPAWI.1714.630xii]

DE NAYAC, LOUIS WILLIAM DUREPAIRE, a Huguenot formerly in military service of the King of Prussia, petitioned for estates on St Kitts by right of his wife the widow of ...Maigne, 1715. [SPAWI. 1715.643]

DE NELL, ..., in Nova Scotia, 1711. [JCTP.1711.673]

DE NEST, Sieur, of Fecamp, from France to Canada , 1630. [CSPC.V]

DENNIE, ..., in St Kitts, 1672. [SPAWI.1672.903]

DE NOISELL, MALLET, master of Le Colombe from Bordeaux to Canada in 1689. [Gironde Archives. 6B1093]

DE NOGEL, Frere PHILLIPE, in St Kitts, 1671, 1673. [SPAWI.1671.583; 1673.1036]

DENTREMONT, CHARLES, and his wife Ann de la Tour, with three sons and one daughter, near Annapolis Royal, 1732; a petition, 1732; in Pobomcoup, Nova Scotia, 1736. [SPAWI.1732.259; 1736.462][JCTP.1732.321]

DENYS, SIMON PIERRE, master of the Bretonne de la Rochelle from La Rochelle bound for Acadia on 8 April 1694. [Charente Maritime Archives, B235/129]

DENYS, ..., in Nova Scotia, 1698. [SPAWI.1698.848ii]

DE PAQUERAY, LOUIS, a planter in Nevis, deceased by 1701. [SPAWI.1701.1091]

DE PARRON DEPELLIERE, LE, Captain, master of Le Fort at Martinique in 1702. [SPAWI.1702.195]

The French in the Americas, 1620-1820

DE PASAR, PAUL, a weaver, with his wife and two children, to emigrate to Virginia, 1621. [CSPC.Addenda; Colonial Correspondence, Vol.i,#45]

DE PAS FEUQUIERS, Sieur Chevalier, Governor and Lieutenant General of the French Windward Islands, 1723. [SPAWI.1723.419]

DE PASLE, Captain, master of L'Orriflame at Martinique, 1702. [SPAWI.1702.195]

DE PASQUIER, ..., to transport Swiss Protestants to Nova Scotia, 1750. [JCTP.1750.151]

DE PEIU, ..., in Quebec, 1711. [JCTP.1711.673]

DE PEN, Le Chevalier, a French officer at the Capture of St John's, Newfoundland, 1709. [SPAWI.1709.890ii]

DE PENNART, Captain FONTENAU, master of a French warship, captured The Fortune of New England, master Thomas Barton, and took them and the crew as prisoners to Isle du Rhe, around 1630. [CSPCol.V.1630.112]

DE PERIER, ..., Governor of Louisiana, 1726. [HLF]

DE POINCY, Chevalier, Governor of St Kitts and Lieutenant General of the French, 1640; 1654. [SPAWI.1730.324][CSPCol.1654.XII]

DE PORACY, Captain, was captured at Mariegalante in 1691. [SPAWI.1737.461]

DE POUY, JEAN, in St Vincent's, 1777. [JCTP.84.69]

DE POYETT, ..., in St Kitts, 1673. [SPAWI.1674.1273]

DE PRADEL, Le Chevalier, Commandant of Fort des Natchez, 1732. [HLF]

DE PRAILLE, ..., in Guadaloupe, 1674. [SPAWI.1674.1333]

DE PRAYLE, ..., in St Kitts, 1672. [SPAWI.1672.903]

DE PRE, JEAN, French refugees, landed in Virginia, 1700. [SPAWI.1700.681]

DE PRESIMON,...... in St Kitts, 1672. [SPAWI.1672.903]

D'ERAIGNY, Marquis, Governor of Martinique, 1691. [SPAWI.1691.1557]

The French in the Americas, 1620-1820

DE RAMSEY, ..., Governor General at Montreal, 1710; 1723. [SPAWI.1710.528vi; 1723.805]

DE RAVINIER, LOUIS FOURNIER, in Grenada, 1769. [JCTP.1769.156]

DE REICHENBACH, FISCHER, member of the Grand Council of Berne, promoter of Swiss emigration to South Carolina, 1722. [SPAWI.1722.378]

DE RESLUS, ANDRES, Governor of St Domingo, 1689. [SPAWI.1689.85i]

DE RICHEBOURG, PHILLIPE, a clergyman in Manikan town, Virginia, 1705. [SPAWI.1705.924i]

DE RICK, JOHN HENRY, was granted 50 acres in Granville County, South Carolina, 1738. [NA.CO5.398]

DERNEVILLE, ..., an army officer with 23 years service in Louisiana by 1759. [Archive des Colonies, serie D, troupes colonials, registres D 2C.50/58]

DE RO, ..., in St Kitts, 1672. [SPAWI.1672.903]

DE ROCQUE, DAVID, a fisherman, captured by the Spanish off Cuba in 1676. [SPAWI.1676.1101]

DE ROCQUEFEUIL, le Comte, in West Indies, 1751. [JCTP.1751.185]

DE ROSSET, JOHN, in Wilmington, North Carolina, 1787. [see will of Louis de Rosset, PCC]

DE ROSSET, LOUIS, in North Carolina, 1752. [JCTP.1752.297]; formerly in North Carolina, died in London, probate 1787, Prerogative Court of Canterbury.

DE ROSSET, ..., master of La Victoire of La Compagnie Francaise D'Occident, when bound from the Mississippi via Havana for France, on 15 May 1719, was captured by HMS Diamond and taken to New York. [SPAWI.1719.343ii]

DERRATSON, JEAN, master of La Fleur du Jour which was captured when bound for Quebec in 1747. [NA.HCA32.112/1]

DE RUAN PALLU, ..., in St Kitts, 1671. [SPAWI.1671.583]

DE SAGULIERS, GABRIEL, in Barbados, died 1768. [GM.38.198]

The French in the Americas, 1620-1820

DE SAINT ANGE, ..., Commandant of of Fort de Chartres, 1730. [HLF]

DE SAINT BASILE, Souer J.M., Lady Superior of the Ursulines in Martinique, 1689. [SPAWI.1689.157ii]

DE SAINT CROY, Marquis, Commandant de Troupes in New France, 1708. [SPAWI.1708.60]

DE SAINT DENIS, ..., Commandant of Fort de Natchitoches, 1731. [HLF]

DE SAINT ESTIENNE, CHARLES, Sieur de la Tour, was granted Acadia by King Louis XIII in 1631, and in 1651 he was appointed Lieutenant General of Acadia, Fort St John, Port de la Tour, etc. [SPAWI.1733.367]

DE SAINT JULIEN, HENRY, was granted 350 acres on Santee River, South Carolina, 1738. [NA.CO5.398]

DE SAINT JULIEN, JAMES, was granted 500 acres on the Santee River, South Carolina, 1737. [NA.CO5.398]

DE SAINT JULIEN, JOSEPH, was granted 500 acres in Berkley County, South Carolina, 1738. [NA.CO5.398]

DE SAINT JULIEN, PAUL, was granted 653 acres in Berkley County, South Carolina, 1738. [NA.CO5.398]

DE SAINT JULIEN, PETER, was granted 1255 acres on the Santee River, South Carolina, 1738. [NA.CO5.398]

DE SAINT LAURENT, Chevalier, in St Kitts, 1671, 1678; at Fort St Pierre, Martinique, 1686. [SPAWI.1671.583; 1678.763; 1686.997vi]

DE SAINT LOUIS, Chevalier, of the Regiment de Bearn, a French soldier captured in Canada, 1759. [SM.21.541]

DE SAINT PIERRE, DUMESNIL, a French Protestant at Cap de Sable, Nova Scotia, 1767. [FPA#7]

DE SAINT PONCY, Father, a Catholic priest in Annapolis Royal, Acadia 1732. [SPAWI.1732.454/455; 1735.462]

DE SALVAYE, ..., at Fort St Louis in Illinois, 1683. [SPAWI.1684.1817i]

The French in the Americas, 1620-1820

DE SALVERT, ANTOINE PERIER, Lieutenant, from Brest, France, to New Orleans with 150 soldiers in 1730. [HLF]

DE SANCE, MARTIN, a French shipmaster at St John's, Newfoundland, 1596. [CSPC.I.8]

DE SANCE, MICHAEL, a French shipmaster at St John's, Newfoundland, 1596. [CSPC.I.8]

DE SANCE, Baron ANTOINE, promoter of a proposed Huguenot emigration to Carolina in 1630. [CSPCol.1630.V.68/69/70/71/72/73/75]

DE SENNE, JAMES, master of the <u>Bonaventure de Dieppe</u>, to St Kitts in 1653; to Jamaica, 1658. [CSPCol:1653.vol.XII][Cal.SPDom.XIII.218]

DESMAGES, ..., in Grenada, 1763. [JCTP.1763.386]

D'ESNAMBUE, ..., in St Kitts, 1625. [SPAWI.1734.314ii]

DE SOUSEUIRE, HENRY, was granted 300 acres in Granville County, South Carolina, 1738. [NA.CO5.398]

DE SPARRE, Madame, from St Domingo, died in London on 15 November 1798. [GM.98.992]

D'ESTIMAUVILLE, Chevalier, from Canada, married Miss Blyth, niece of J. Betts, in Boston, Lincolnshire, on 3 June 1796. [GM.66.523]

DETCHEGOYEN, ..., from Cape Francois to Charleston, South Carolina, aboard the <u>Two Friends of Boston</u>, 1723. [SPAWI.1724.85ii]

DE TROYES, ..., Commandant of Fort Niagara, 1688-1692. [HLF]

DE VILER, Mrs GRACE, born 1711, died in Jamaica 1791. [GM.61.1065]

DE VISION, PETER ABRAM, was granted 50 acres in Granville County, South Carolina, 1738. [NA.CO5.398]

DE VRILL, LEWIS, was granted 50 acres in Granville County, South Carolina, 1738. [NA.CO5.398]

DELMESTRE, FRANCIS, in Dominica, 1772. [JCTP.1772.319]

The French in the Americas, 1620-1820

DELMESTRE, PIERRE, in Dominica, 1772. [JCTP.1772.319]

DE NELL, JOHN, in Nova Scotia, 1763. [JCTP.1711.673]

DE ROSEMOND, PAUL, a French Protestant, petitioned to be shipped to America, possibly went to Jamaica, 1682. [SPAWI.1682.883]

DE SALVAYE, Sieur, in Canada, 1684. [SPAWI.1684.1817]

DESBAT, JOHN, in Carriacou, 1771. [JCTP.1771.244]

DESBAT, LEWIS, in Carriacou, 1771. [JCTP.1771.244]

DES BOIS, JEAN, master of Marguerite de la Rochelle from France to Acadia in 1664. [Charente Maritime Archives, #B5615]

DE PAS FEUQUIERES, ..., Governor of Martinique and the French Leeward Islands, 1721. [SPAWI.1721.501viii]

DE SAINT JULIEN, HENRY, land grants on the Santee River and in Granville County, South Carolina, in 1738. [SPAWI.1738.280]

DE SAINT JULIEN, JOSEPH, land grant in Berkley County, South Carolina, in 1738. [SPAWI.1738.280]

DE SAINT JULIEN, PAUL, land grant in Berkley County, South Carolina, in 1738. [SPAWI.1738.280]

DE SAINT JULIEN, PETER, land grants on the Santee River, South Carolina, in 1738. [SPAWI.1738.280]

DE SAINT PONCY, ..., a Roman Catholic priest at Annapolis Royal, 1734. [SPAWI.1734.164iv]

DE SALLE, FRANCOIS, a French Indian at St John's River, Nova Scotia, a letter 10 November 1720. [SPAWI.1720.298ii]

DES BARBES, ESTIENNE, master of La Concorde a privateer which was captured when bound for the West Indies in 1747. [NA.HCA32.102/2]

DESCONTES, ..., a merchant at Canso, Canada, 1719. [SPAWI.1719.208ii]

The French in the Americas, 1620-1820

DESENDRE, ANTHOIN, a laborer, with his wife and one child, to emigrate to Virginia, 1621. [CSPC.Addenda; Colonial Correspondence, Vol.i,#45]

DE SENNE, JAMES, master of Bonaventure de Dieppe, to St Kitts in 1653; to Jamaica in 1658. [CSPCol.XII][Cal.SPDom.XIII.218]

DE SERBIE, Captain, master of Le Pesselant at Martinique in 1702. [SPAWI.1702.195]

DE SEREL, Marquis, Governor of Santa Domingo and Liggan, letters, 1720. [SPAWI.1721.527]

DES GROSILIERS, ..., in Hudson Bay Company Service, 1667-1668. [SPAWI.1683.2097]

DES HERBIERS, ..., Governor of Louisbourg, 1749, 1752. [JCTP.1749.465; 1752.303]

DES MAGES, ..., in Grenada. 1763. [JCTP.18763.386]

DE SOUSEUIRE, HENRY, land grant in Granville County, South Carolina, in 1738. [SPAWI.1738.280]

DE POUNCEY, ..., French Governor of Hispaniola, 1682. [SPAWI.1682.769]

DE SHOLOINE, Captain, at Fort Sorel, Quebec, 1711. [JCTP.1711.673]

DESNELL, DU PLESSIS, ..., in St Vincent, 1772. [JCTP.1772.319]

DES NOYERS, ..., an army officer, killed by the Chicachas at Fort Saint Claude in 1730. [HLF]

D'ESTREES, Count, Admiral of the French squadron in the West Indies, 1676. [SPAWI.1683.2089]

DE SUBERCASE, ..., Governor of Placentia and Port Royal, 1708, 1711; French governor of Acadia, 1717; 1719, 1728. [JCTP.1711.673; 1717.350] [SPAWI.1708.60/391/554i; 1719.236; 1728.229]

DE POINCY, ..., Governor of St Kitts, 1640. [SPAWI.1730.324]

DE RETHEUILLE, BINOIST, in Guadaloupe, 1703. [SPAWI.1705.1025ii]

The French in the Americas, 1620-1820

DE RIDEAUX, CORNEILLE, master of Le Pere de Famille de Rochelle which was captured when bound from the West Indies in 1747. [NA.HCA32.145]

DES RUAUX, ..., in St Lucia (?) 1731. [SPAWI.1731.248]

DE SAINT CASTEEN, Baron, in Canada, 1711. [JCTP.1711.673]

DE SAINT DENIS, LOUIS JUCHEREAU, born 1676 in Quebec, explorer of the Mississippi Valley, died 1744. [HLF]

DE SAINT ESTIENNE, CHARLES, at Port Royal, a letter, 9 October 1629. [NRS.GD22.3.581][SPAWI.1699.108]

DES BARBES, ..., master of La Perle which was captured hen bound for the West Indies in 1747. [NA.HCA32.145]

DE SEREL, Marquis, Governor of Hispaniola, 1721. [JCTP.1721.286]

DE SPOT, NICOLAS, master of Marie from La Rochelle to Acadia and the West Indies in 1685. [Charente Maritime Archives, B56837]

DE SUBERCASSE, ..., Governor of Placentia, Newfoundland, 1706, 1710, 1712. [JCTP.1705.145/204/206; 1725.168; 1728.414/415] [SPAWI.1712.166; 1725.609c]

DES VAUX, MICHEL, master of a French Newfoundland fishery ship Le Pierre Andre which was captured in 1744. [NA.HCA32.143/1]

DETCHART, MARSAM, master of St Paul , a Newfoundland fisheries ship, which was captured in 1744. [NA.HCA32.142/1]

DETCHEVERRY, MICHAEL, master of La Vierge de la Rochelle from La Rochelle to Newfoundland in 1677. [La Rochelle Archives, Teuleron, 50]

DETCHIVERY, ..., master of a French vessel belonging to Cape Francois arrived at Boston in June 1718; merchant at Cape Francois trading to Charleston, South Carolina, 1723. [SPAWI.1719.52v; 1724.85iii]

DE TOZON, Lieutenant, of Guienne, a French soldier captured in Canada, 1759. [SM.21.541]

The French in the Americas, 1620-1820

DE TRACY, ..., from La Rochelle with seven ships and 1500 passengers and soldiers bound for the Caribbean and Canada in March 1664. [CSPC.1664.891]

DE TROU, JAN, a Walloon wool carder, with his wife and five children, to emigrate to Virginia, 1621. [CSPC.Addenda; Colonial Correspondence, Vol.i,#45]

DE VAINE, Captain, master of Le Trydent at Martinique, 1702. [SPAWI.1702.195]

DE VAUDEREUIL, PHILLIPPE DE RIGOU, Marquis, Governor of Quebec, 1708, 1710, 1712. [SPAWI.1708.60; 1710.528; 1712.31/116/164, etc]

DE VAUDREUIL, ..., in Canada, 1722; 1723; dead by December 1726. [SPAWI.1723.805; 1732.259; 1726.362]

DE VAUDREUIL, RIGAUD, and his wife, claim to a trading post at Baye de Puants, Quebec, 1767. [JCTP.1767.14]

DE VAUDREUIL, Marquis, Governor of Louisiana, 1743. [HLF]

DE VEAUX, ANDREW, was granted 1350 acres on Saltcatcher River, South Carolina, 1737. [NA.CO5.398]

DE VELLE,........, an army officer with 27 years service in Louisiana by 1759. [Archive des Colonies, serie D, troupes colonials, registres D 2C.50/58]

DE VESESIEN, MARIE MADELAINE GREAUX, in St Vincent, 1772. [JCTP.1772.280]

DE VIGNE, ..., in Guadaloupe, 1681. [SPAWI.1681.190]

DE VILLEBON, ..., Governor of Acadia, 1694;1698. [SPAWI.1694.1136/1143/1320; 1698.912/922/986/988/1082; 1709.554]

DE VILLEPARS, Sieur, commander of the Mazarin, the San Sebastien, the Petite Infante, Belle Isle, and Aurora sent by the French king to the French islands in the America, 1671. [SPAWI.1671.638]

DE VILLETTE, CHARLES LOUIS, a French minister, possibly in St Kitts, 1728. [FPA#277]

The French in the Americas, 1620-1820

DE VILLEAU, Captain, a prisoner in Boston, New England, 1698. [SPAWI.1698.622viii]

DE VILLIERS, Le Sieur, an infantry captain at Fort Duquesnes, Ohio, 1754. [HLF]

DE VISION, PETER ABRAM, land grant in Granville County, South Carolina, in 1738. [SPAWI.1738.280]

DE VOCONNU, PAUL MIGNOT, in Grenada, 1770. [JCTP.1770.180]

DE VOURS, ..., of la Sarre, a French soldier captured in Canada, 1759. [SM.21.541]

DE VOWSERY, FRANCIS, a winegrower, granted land in Carolina, 1683. [SPAWI.1683.1017]

DE VRILL, LOUIS, land grant in Granville County, South Carolina, in 1738. [SPAWI.1738.280]

DE WIGNACOURT, Marquis, petitioned for a settlement for French Protestants in North America, 20 May 1717. [JCTP.1717.233]

DE ZARDRE, CHARLES, born 1705, a bricklayer from Boulogne, bound from London to Maryland as an indentured servant in 1724. [CLRO]

DIGAUD, BARTHELEMY, a sawyer, with his wife and eight children, to emigrate to Virginia, 1621. [CSPC.Addenda; Colonial Correspondence, Vol.i,#45]

DOBREE, THOMAS, co-owner of the Two Friends a brig which was condemned by the Vice Admiralty of Quebec on 17 October 1764 on a charge of smuggling wine. [APCCol.1765.610]

D'OBBEVILLE, LAWRENCE, a surgeon in Nova Scotia, 1752. [JCTP.1752.317]

DOMINICK, JOHN, was granted 50 acres in Granville County, South Carolina, 1738. [NA.CO5.398]

D'OGERON, ..., Governor of Tortuga, 1671. [SPAWI.1671.638]

DORIDAN, JACQUES, master of the Arman de Souder from Chevelet on the River Bordeaux to Newfoundland in 1673. [APCCol.1674/975]

The French in the Americas, 1620-1820

DOSQUEL, ..., Bishop of Quebec, 1732. [SPAWI.1732.454]

DOSSETT, JEAN, master of Hermin de Nantes from France bound for Martinique, captured by the English in 1701. [SPAWI.1701.1192; 1702.8]

DOUPNOY, JEAN, in St Vincent's, 1777. [JCTP.84.69]

DOYER. LOUIS, master of the Count de Paix, bound from St Domingo for Havre de Grace, France, in September 1713, was grounded near the island of Henegua. [SPAWI.1716.247i]

DU AN, J., a French inhabitant of Annapolis Royal, Nova Scotia, 1720. [SPAWI.1720.180xi/xii]

DU BERRY, Councillor of Montserrat, 1779. [JCTP.86.234]

DU BOIS, CHARLES, in Dominica, 1776. [JCTP.83.35]

DU BOIS, JEAN PIERRE, in Grenada, 1769. [JCTP.1769.156]

DU BOIS, JOHN, master of the St Ann of Guadaloupe, seized for smuggling in Antigua, 1730. [APCCol.1730.201]

DU BOIS, JOHN ARMAND, in Wilmington, North Carolina, 1787. [see will of Louis de Rosset, PCC]

DU BOURNAY, JOSEPH, master of La Diane which was captured when bound from the West Indies in 1746. [NA.HCA32.104/2]

DU BRAUIL, ..., residing on the River St John, Acadia, dead by 1718. [SPAWI.1718.789iv]

DU BOIS, THOMAS, in St Michael's, Barbados, died at sea, probate 1699 Prerogative Court of Canterbury

DU CARRETT, JOHANIS, at Collonet, St Mary's, Newfoundland, 1680. [SPAWI.1680.1471]

DU CASSE, ..., a merchant at Petit Guavas, 1698. [SPAWI.1699.45]

DUCHE, ANDREW, was granted 150 acres in Granville County, South Carolina, 1738. [NA.CO5.398]

The French in the Americas, 1620-1820

DU BART, PETER, "the greatest Protestant French merchant in Canada", died 1767. [GM.37.524]

DU CASSE, ..., at Martinique, 1707. [JCTP.1707.455]

DUCHE, ANDREW, land grant in Granville County, South Carolina, in 1738. [SPAWI.1738.280]

DU CHESNAY, ..., in Quebec, a petition, 1765. [JCTP.1765.224]

DU DOIT, GABRIEL, master of La Ville de Nantes which was captured when bound from the West Indies in 1745. [NA.HCA32.156/1]

DU FAUX, GABRIEL, master of La Jeune Marie which was captured when bound from the West Indies in 1745. [NA.HCA32.123]

DU FILHOU, ..., in St Domingo, a letter, 1763. [JCTP.1763.386]

DU FOUR, JEAN, master of La Toison d'Or which was captured when bound for the West Indies in 1745. [NA.HCA32.155]

DU FOUR, THEODORE, a draper, with his wife and two children, to emigrate to Virginia, 1621. [CSPC.Addenda; Colonial Correspondence, Vol.i,#45]

DU FOUS, FRANCOIS, master of L'Hercule which was captured when bound for the West Indies in 1747. [NA.HCA32.117]

DU FRESNAY, ANNE, in Jamaica, 1744. [APCCol.]

DU GUE, PIERRE, master of Le Prophete Samuel which was captured when bound for the West Indies in 1744. [NA.HCA32.142/1]

DU JARDAIN, PRILLEUX, in St Vincent, 1773. [JCTP.1773.334]

DU MAINE, Madam, a planter in Fig Tree Quarter, St Kitts, before 1717. [JCTP.1717.261]

DU MARESQ, PHILLIP, a mariner in Boston, 1720. [SPAWI.1720.22i]

DUMAS, JEROME, French refugees, landed in Virginia, 1700. [SPAWI.1700.681]

DUMAY, CLAUDE DUVAL, in St Vincent, 1771. [JCTP.1771.274]

The French in the Americas, 1620-1820

DUMONT, ..., a French Protestant, petitioned to be shipped to America, possibly went to Jamaica, 1682. [SPAWI.1682.883]

DU MONT, ANTOINE FRANCOIS, master of Le Charon a privateer, which was captured when bound for the West Indies in 1747. [NA.HCA32.100/1]

DU MOUCHE, ..., in St Kitts, 1671. [SPAWI.1671.583]

DU MOY, ..., town major of Montreal, 1708. [SPAWI.1708.60]

DUON, JOHN, rent collector, Annapolis Royal, Nova Scotia, 1734. [SPAWI.1734.164i]

DU PALLAY, Captain, master of Le Firm at Martinique in 1702. [SPAWI.1702.195]

DU PARQUET, ..., Governor of Martinique, 1640. [SPAWI.1730.324]

DU PAS, ..., a civil and criminal judge in St Kitts, 1679. [SPAWI.1679.963]

DU PEUX, JACQUES, master of Saint Pierre de Bordeaux from Bordeaux to Quebec in 1689. [Bordeaux Archives, Ferrand.72; Gironde Archives, 6B73/118, 6B1063]

DU PIN, LOUIS, French refugees, landed in Virginia, 1700. [SPAWI.1700.681]

DU PISSENCOUR, Captain, master of Le Dauphin at Martinique in 1702. [SPAWI.1702.195]

DU PLESSIS, GOSELIN, in St Vincent, 1772. [JCTP.1772.319]

DU PON, MICHEL, a hatter, with his wife and two children, to emigrate to Virginia, 1621. [CSPC.Addenda; Colonial Correspondence, Vol.i,#45]

DU PONCEAU, FAVRY, at the Baye de Phillipeaux, Labrador, 1764. [JCTP.1764.219]

DU PONT, ABRAHAM, was granted 500 acres in Berkley County, South Carolina, 1737. [NA.CO5.398]

The French in the Americas, 1620-1820

DU PONT, GIDEON, was granted 400 acres in Berkley County, South Carolina, 1737. [NA.CO5.398]; in Charleston, South Carolina, probate 1788, Prerogative Court of Canterbury.

DU PONT, GIDEON, a merchant in Charleston, died 1785. [GM.55.489]

DU PONT DE NEMOURS, ..., died in Elantekenan, Wilmington, Delaware, 10 August 1817. [GM.87.376]

DU PORT, STEPHEN, in St Kitts, 1698; 1714. [SPAWI.1698.675; [APCCol.1714.1069][JCTP.1707.467][SPAWI.1714.630]

DU PORTAIL, LOUIS JOSEPH LE BECQUE, born in France, a Major General in the American Revolution, died on passage from New York to Havre de Grace, France, aboard the Sophia of New York, 11 August 1801. [GM.71.960]

DU PRE, CORNELIUS, was granted 1383 acres in Berkley County, South Carolina, 1737. [NA.CO5.398]

DU QUE, FRANCOIS, master of La Jeune Monarque which was captured when bound for the West Indies in 1748. [NA.HCA32.118/2]

DU QUESNE, ..., Governor of Martinique, 1715, 1716. [SPAWI.1715.244i/439/654iii/etc] [JCTP.1716.206]

DU QUESNE, ..., Governor of Canada, letters, 1752. [JCTP.1752.399]

DU QUESNELL, ..., Governor of Louisbourg, 1744. [JCTP.1744.133/137]

DU RAMSAY, ..., Governor of Montreal, 1708. [SPAWI.1708.60]

DU RAND, ALAIN, master of Marie de la Rochelle from France to Canada and the West Indies in 1690; master of L'Industrie de la Rochelle from La Rochelle to Quebec and the West Indies in 1694. [Charente Maritime Archives, 6B74.10; 6B295.115; B5710]

DU RAND, JEAN, master of Le Diligente de la Rochelle from La Rochelle to Quebec and the West Indies in 1685, from La Rochelle to Chedabouctou in 1686, from La Rochelle to Quebec in 1687 also in 1688. [Gironde Archives B72.158; Charente Maritime Archives B5681.83.85; La Rochelle Archives; Bilbiotheque Nationale, Paris, Collection Arnoul 21443]

The French in the Americas, 1620-1820

DU RAND, Father JUSTINIEN, in Recollet, Annapolis Royal, Nova Scotia, 1720. [SPAWI.1720.180iii/iv]

DU RAND, PIERRE, master of La Ville de Lisbonne de la Rochelle from La Rochelle to Quebec and the West Indies in 1684; master of Saint Francois de la Rochelle from La Rochelle to Quebec and the West Indies in 1687; master of St Francois de Paul de la Rochelle from La Rochelle via Bordeaux to Quebec and Martinique in 1690. [Charente Maritime Archives, B5682; B235.139; 6B74.14]

DU RAND, Father, a French Catholic priest in Nova Scotia, 1720. [SPAWI.1720.180ix]

DU RAND, ..., in Acadia, 1750. [JCTP.1750.120/123]

DU RANT, ..., late chaplain of the fort at Carcony, New York, 1721. [JCTP.1721.317]

DU REPAIRE, ..., and his wife the widow of M. Maigne, planters of Le Jardin, La Solovette, and La Frontiere, in St Kitts, 1715. [JCTP.1715.85]

DU RET, JEAN, master of Suzanne de la Rochelle from La Rochelle to Newfoundland in 1688; master of La Fille Bien Aymee de la Rochelle from France to Quebec and the West Indies in 1693. [Charente Maritime Archives, B235/162; B5687/8]

DU ROUSSEAU, J., vestryman of St Michael's, Barbados, 1719. [SPAWI.1719.356xxx]

DU ROUSSEAU, Colonel, storekeeper in Barbados, 1728, 1728. [JCTP.1728.394; 1729.40]

DU ROY, ANTHONY, a planter on St Kitts, 1712. [JCTP]

DUSSEAU, JOSEPH, a pilot of Isle du Pas, Montreal, 1786. [NA.AO13.24.136]

DU TARTRE, DANIEL, guilty of murdering Captain Peter Simmons, in South Carolina, reprieved 12 October 1724. [SPAWI.1724.388v]

DU TARTE, FRANCOIS, French refugees, landed in Virginia, 1700. [SPAWI.1700.681]

The French in the Americas, 1620-1820

DU TARTRE, JOHN, guilty of murdering Captain Peter Simmons, in South Carolina, reprieved 12 October 1724. [SPAWI.1724.388v]

DU TARTRE, PETER, guilty of murdering Captain Peter Simmons, in South Carolina, 1724. [SPAWI.1724.388v]

DU THAIS, DANIEL, a land grant in South Carolina, 1689. [SPAWI.1689.652]

DU TILLY, Sieur, in Renous, Newfoundland, 1703; a prisoner in Newfoundland, July 1704. [SPAWI.1704.315c/i][JCTP. 1704.28/29]

DU TISNE, Captain CLAUDE CHARLES, explorer of Kansas, Missouri and Oklahoma, 1719. [HLF]

DU TOY, FRANCOIS, French refugee, landed in Virginia, 1700. [SPAWI.1700.681]

DU VALL, JOSIAH, died in Barbados, probate 1694 Prerogative Court of Canterbury

DU VERGES,........., an army officer with 39 years service in Louisiana by 1759. [Archive des Colonies, serie D, troupes colonials, registres D 2C.50/58]

DU VIVE, ..., an army officer, from Quebec to Cape Breton, 1713. [SPAWI.1713.522]

DU VIVIER, PHILIPE, French refugee, landed in Virginia, 1700. [SPAWI.1700.681]

EGRON, NICOLAS, master of St Louis from La Rochelle to Quebec, 1693. [Gironde Archives, 6B76/95]

ELIZARD, ABRAHAM, was granted 800 acres in Granville County, South Carolina, 1737. [NA.CO5.398]

ENDERTIN, HENRY, was granted 200 acres in Granville County, South Carolina, 1738. [NA.CO5.398][SPAWI.1738.280]

ENGLIN, HENRY, was granted lot 183 in Purrysburgh, Granville County, South Carolina, 1738. [NA.CO5.398]

The French in the Americas, 1620-1820

ENOUF, NICHOLAS, of Guernsey, master of the brig Two Friends condemned by the Vice Admiralty Court of Quebec, 17 October 1764, guilty of smuggling wine. [APCCol.1765.610]

ESCOUBET, ..., master of the L'Aimable Marie from La Rochelle on 23 October 1714 bound for Cuba, after unloading part of the cargo at St Domingoit was seized by ships from Jamaica. [SPAWI.1718.591ii]

ESTELLE, PIERRE, master of the Saint Joseph from Tortuga bound for Lisbon or La Rochelle in 1670, but landed in Boston, New England. [SPAWI.1672.1007]

ESTIENNE, ..., a partly French Indian in Cape Breton, 1720. [SPAWI.1720.241ii]

EVEQUE, ..., in Quebec, 1732. [SPAWI.1732.454]

FABARY, RICHARD, master of La Fidele which was captured when bound rom the West Indies in 1744. [NA.HCA32.111/1]

FALLETT, ABRAHAM, was granted 400 acres in Granville County, South Carolina, 1738. [NA.CO5.398]

FALLOU, J., master of the Mariage Royale de la Rochelle from La Rochelle to Cape Breton in 1662. [La Rochelle Library, Cherbonnier ms]

FANERIL, BENJAMIN, in New York, co-owner of the Rhode Island built sloop Good Intent, 1717. [JCTP.1717.437]

FAREY, JEAN, French refugee, landed in Virginia, 1700. [SPAWI.1700.681]

FARNARCQUE, THOMAS, a locksmith, with his wife and seven children, to emigrate to Virginia, 1621. [CSPC.Addenda; Colonial Correspondence, Vol.i,#45]

FAUCHER, ..., at Montserrat, 1736. [SPAWI.1736.460]

FAURE, DANIEL, and two children, French refugees, landed in Virginia, 1700. [SPAWI.1700.681]

The French in the Americas, 1620-1820

FAURE, JEAN, master of Le Dauphin de la Rochelle from Bordeaux to Newfoundland, Canada, and the West Indies, 1695. [Charente Maritime Archives, B5691]

FAURE, alias LA PLANTE, JEAN, in Placentia, Newfoundland, 1706. [JCTP.1725.168] [SPAWI.1725.609c]

FAURE, the widow, and four children, French refugees, landed in Virginia, 1700. [SPAWI.1700.681]

FEBURES, LOUIS, born 1705, a laborer, bound from London to Maryland as an indentured servant in 1724. [CLRO]

FELICIEN, Father, a French Catholic priest on Grenada, 1793. [FPA#291]

FELIX, Father, a French Catholic priest at MiNRS, Annapolis Royal, Nova Scotia, 1718; 1720. [SPAWI.1718.565ii/iii; 1720.180xvi/371I]

FERRET, ANDRE, master of Le Don de Dieu a Newfoundland fishery ship, which was captured in 1745. [NA.HCA32.106]

FERRIER, PIERRE, wife and child, French refugees, landed in Virginia, 1700. [SPAWI.1700.681]

FILLYE, PIERRE, master of Noir van Holland from Dieppe to Quebec in 1664. [La Rochelle Archives, Cherbonnier ms]

FLANDRIN, JOHN CHARLES, in Grenada, 1769. [JCTP.1769.156]

FLEURISSON, THOMAS, master of Louis Marie de la Rochelle from France to Quebec in 1688. [La Rochelle Library, Berthellot pp; Gironde Archives, 6B72.153, 6B294/19; 6B1056]

FLEWRY, ELIZABETH, French refugees, landed in Virginia, 1700. [SPAWI.1700.681]

FLIT, MARIE, and her husband, a miller, with their two children, to emigrate to Virginia, 1621. [CSPC.Addenda; Colonial Correspondence, Vol.i,#45]

FLUSIAN, PETER, owner of the sloop Dolphin in Bridgetown, Barbados, 1699. [SPAWI.1699.476ii]

The French in the Americas, 1620-1820

FOREST, RENY, a farmer near Annapolis Royal, Nova Scotia, 1734. [SPAWI.1734.164i]

FORNICHON, ..., settled in Jamaica, 1754. [JCTP.1754.66/106]

FOUCAUD, FRANCOIS, master of the privateer Le Royal Phillipe which was captured when bound for the West Indies in 1748. [NA.HCA32.150]

FOUCHER, ..., at the Baye de Phillipeaux, Labrador, 1764. [JCTP.1764.219]

FOUCHIE, JEAN, French refugees, landed in Virginia, 1700. [SPAWI.1700.681]

FOUDIRNIER, PAUL, a merchant in St Kitts, died 1 August 1770. [GM.40.393]

FOUDRIN, FRANCOIS, a leather dresser, a young man, to emigrate to Virginia, 1621. [CSPC.Addenda; Colonial Correspondence, Vol.i,#45]

FOUGERON, PIERRE, master of Izaac et Marie de la Rochelle from La Rochelle to Quebec and the West Indies in 1686. [Gironde Archives, 6B71/160; 6B291/131]

FOUNTAIN, JOHN, was granted 150 acres in Granville County, South Carolina, 1737. [NA.CO5.398]

FOURNIER, PROSPER, in Grenada, 1769. [JCTP.1769.156]

FOUSSE, JEAN, French refugees, landed in Virginia, 1700. [SPAWI.1700.681]

FOUSSIER, PHILIP, born in La Rochelle, a Protestant, residing in Barbados, became a free denizen of England, 1669. [SPAWI.1669.102]

FRAISE, CATHERINE, a Huguenot and planter at Cabesterre, St Kitts, around 1695, daughter of Daniel de Lompre, a petition, 1714; estates restored in 1715. [APCCol.1715.1225] [SPAWI.1714.630xiii; 1715.375]

FRAMERIE, MARTIN, a musician, with his wife and one child, to emigrate to Virginia, 1621. [CSPC.Addenda; Colonial Correspondence, Vol.i,#45]

FRANCHOMME, CHARLES, land grant in Carolina, 1685. [SPAWI.1686.132]

The French in the Americas, 1620-1820

FRANCOIS, CHARLES, master of <u>Sainte Famille de la Rochelle</u> from La Rochelle to Canada and the West Indies in 1690. [Gironde Archives, 6B74.18; La Rochelle Archives, Martin ms]

FRETT, ELISIAS, born in France, 1678, aboard the <u>Anne and Katherine,</u> from New York via Maryland bound for London in 1690. [NA.HCA.Rex v. The Anne and Katherine, 1692]

FROMENTIN, JEAN, master of <u>La Belle Louise de Bordeaux</u>, a privateer, captured when bound from the West Indies in 1745. [NA.HCA32.98/3]

FRUIOU, G., at Quebec, July 1666. [CSPC.1666.1229]

GABERET, ..., in the West Indies, 1680. [SPAWI.1680.1437]

GABIOU, ISAAC, master of <u>Le Roue de Fortune</u> from La Rochelle to Quebec and Newfoundland in 1695. [Charente Maritime Archives, B5691][La Rochelle Archives, Gariteau ms]

GAIGNEUR, PIERRE, master of <u>Le Soleil de la Rochelle</u> from Bordeaux to Quebec and the West Indies in 1680. [Gironde Archives, 6B68/16]

GAILLARD, JEAN, and his son, French refugees, landed in Virginia, 1700. [SPAWI.1700.681]

GALLIFAIT, ..., Lieutenant Governor of Montreal, 1708, at the town of Trois Rivieres, 1711. [SPAWI.1708.60] [JCTP.1711.673]

GANTOIS, P., a student of theology, a young man, to emigrate to Virginia, 1621. [CSPC.Addenda; Colonial Correspondence, Vol.i,#45]

GARBAY, JACQUES, master of <u>Le Rostan</u> which was captured when bound for the West Indies in 1744. [NA.HCA32.150]

GARESCHE, JEAN, master of <u>La Famille de la Rochelle</u> from France to Quebec and Newfoundland in 1691. [Charente Maritime Archives, B5687/88]

GARIGNE, MATTHEW, ain St Kitts, 1712. [JCTP.1712.395]

GARRAUD, JEAN, master of the schooner <u>Romaine de Martinique</u>, at Barbados, 1725. [SPAWI.1725.398]

GARRET, ..., in Guadaloupe, 1724, 1725. [SPAWI.1724.400; 1728.65]

GASPAR, PIERRE, to emigrate to Virginia, 1621. [CSPC.Addenda; Colonial Correspondence, Vol.i,#45]

GASTINAUS, FRANCIS, born in La Rochelle, France, 1666, boatswain aboard the Anne and Katherine, from New York via Maryland bound for London in 1690. [NA.HCA.Rex v. The Anne and Katherine, 1692]

GAULIN, ANTOINE, a priest at St John's River, Nova Scotia, a letter, missionary among the natives of Acadia and Isle Royalle, 1722. [JCTP.1722.384][SPAWI.1722.205/209]

GAULTIER, Lieutenant ZACHARIAH, court-martialled in Jamaica for abusing a superior officer, 1692. [SPAWI.1692.2064]

GAURY, JEAN, wife and child, French refugees, landed in Virginia, 1700. [SPAWI.1700.681]

GAURY, PIERRE, wife and child, French refugees, landed in Virginia, 1700. [SPAWI.1700.681]

GAYRIN, ALEXIS, in St Vincent, 1773. [JCTP.1773.334]

GAYRIN, PIERRE, in St Vincent, 1773. [JCTP.1773.334]

GENTET, JAMES, in St Johns, Newfoundland, 1730. [SPAWI.1730.503iv]

GENTET, PIERRE, master of the L'Aigle Noir de la Rochelle from La Rochelle to Quebec in 1676, and to Quebec and the West Indies in 1677. [La Rochelle Municipal Library ms]; master of La Rochelaise de la Rochelle from La Rochelle to Newfoundland in 1680. [Charente Maritime Archives, B5679]

GERMON, JEAN, master of the L'Aimable de la Rochelle from La Rochelle to Canada in 1691. [Charente Maritime Archives ms]

GHISELIN, CLAUDE, a tailor, a young man, to emigrate to Virginia, 1621. [CSPC.Addenda; Colonial Correspondence, Vol.i,#45]

GIBAULT, JACQUES, master of Les Deux Freres which was captured when bound from the West Indies in 1745. [NA.HCA32.104/1]

The French in the Americas, 1620-1820

GIGNILIATT, JOHN, was granted 500 acres in Berkley County, South Carolina, 1738. [NA.CO5.398][SPAWI.1738.280]

GIGONS, MAGDALAIN, French refugees, landed in Virginia, 1700. [SPAWI.1700.681]

GILLE, JAN, a Walloon laborer, with his wife and three children, to emigrate to Virginia, 1621. [CSPC.Addenda; Colonial Correspondence, Vol.i,#45]

GILLEBER, ..., in Curacao, a letter, 19 January 1709. [SPAWI.1709.411i]

GILLET, JEAN MARIE, master of Le Telemaque which was captured when bound from the West Indies in 1748. [NA.HCA32.155]

GIRARD, PETER, a Huguenot in Carolina, 1699. [SPAWI.1699.183]

GIRAUDEL, PIERRE, master of Le Paschal which was captured when bound from the West Indies in 1746. [NA.HCA32.142/1]

GIRAULT, JEAN BAPTISTE, in Dominica, 1772. [JCTP.1772.319]

GIRAURDEAU, PIERRE, master of L'Esprit du Bois D'Olonne from Newfoundland bound for France in 1676. [[APCCol.1676.1105]

GIRON, FRANCOIS, master of Le Bolton du Cap a privateer, which was captured when bound from the West Indies in 1748. [NA.HCA32.98/2]

GIRROIZ, JAMES, a farmer near Annapolis Royal, Nova Scotia, 1734. [SPAWI.1734.164i]

GODART, MARM., in St Lucia, 1730. [SPAWI.1730.260.v/vi]

GODET, BERNARD, a fisherman in Annapolis Royal, Nova Scotia, 1714; 1727. [SPAWI.1715.568iv; 1727.789][JCTP.1715.71]

GODET, DENIS, a fisherman in Annapolis Royal, Nova Scotia, 1714. [SPAWI.1715.568iv][JCTP.1715.71]

GODET, GILLIAM, piloted the Indian attack on Canso, Nova Scotia, 1723. [SPAWI.1725.718viii]

The French in the Americas, 1620-1820

GODIN, BENJAMIN, co-owner of the Carolina a frigate, merchant in Charleston, South Carolina, 1724. [SPAWI.1724.85]; a land grants on the Santee and Combee Rivers, South Carolina, in 1738. [SPAWI.1738.281]

GODIN, DANIEL, a resident of New Brunswick, 1786. [NA.AO13.80.325]

GODINEAU, Lieutenant S., on Captain Dongan's Expedition at Albany, New York, pre 1690. [SPAWI.1690.886]

GODRIOT, CATHARINE, French refugees, landed in Virginia, 1700. [SPAWI.1700.681]

GOGANE, DOMINIQUE, born 1699 in Paris, a painter, an indentured servant bound from London to Maryland in 1719. [CLRO]

GOILLARD, ETIENNE, from La Rochelle, France, aboard the St Joseph, to Tortuga, in 1670. [SPAWI.1672.1007]

GOLINE, ..., a missionary in Cape Breton and Cape Sables, 1713. [SPAWI.1713.522]

GONSON, SIMON, master of La Marie Victorie, confiscated by the Court of the Vice Admiralty of Barbados, 1729. [APCCol.1729.187]

GONTHIER, DAVID, and wife, French refugees, landed in Virginia, 1700. [SPAWI.1700.681]

GORDEAU, ..., an Indian agent in Canada, 1704. [SPAWI.1704.455]

GOSSELIN, FRANCOIS, in Quebec, a deposition, 1763. [JCTP.1763.308]

GOUDALIE, ..., a priest in Nova Scotia, letters 1732. [JCTP.1732.321]

GOUDIER, BERNARD, in Beau-Bassin, Nova Scotia, later in South Carolina, 1756. [JCTP.1756.226]

GOUGEON, GREGORY, a land grant in New York, 1715. [SPAWI.1715.297]

GOULINE, ..., a priest in Nova Scotia, letters 1732. [JCTP.1732.321]

GOULINE, ..., at Les Mines, Nova Scotia, 1732. [SPAWI.1732.259]

GOUNON, PIERRE, in Massachusetts, a letter, 1753. [JCTP.1753.465]

The French in the Americas, 1620-1820

GOURDEMAN, JEAN, a laborer, with his wife and five children, to emigrate to Virginia, 1621. [CSPC.Addenda; Colonial Correspondence, Vol.i,#45]

GOURDEAUX, ..., in Nova Scotia, 1720. [SPAWI.1720.298i]

GRANIER, JOHN, was granted 800 acres in Granville County, South Carolina, 1738. [NA.CO5.398][SPAWI.1738.281]

GRAVOIL, PIERRE, master of La Renee Marie de St Gilles from La Rochelle to Acadia and the West Indies in 1684. [Charente Maritime Archives, B5682]

GREAUX, JACQUES, in St Vincent, 1773. [JCTP.1773.334]

GRELET, PIERRE, French refugee, landed in Virginia, 1700. [SPAWI.1700.681]

GRENIER, ANTOINE, a gardener, with his wife, to emigrate to Virginia, 1621. [CSPC.Addenda; Colonial Correspondence, Vol.i,#45]

GREYSOLON, DANIEL, sieur Du Luth, born in France 1636, explorer, died in Canada, 171o.[HLF]

GRIVOIS, PIERRE, at Les Mines, Nova Scotia, 1732. [SPAWI.1732.152]

GUEGUEN DE GUEGUEN, TUGE, master of Le Comte de Virlade which was captured when bound from the West Indies around 1746. [NA.HCA32.100/2]

GUERARD, JACOB, a gentleman of Normandy, petitioned for ships to transport 80 Huguenot families to Carolina, 1679.(they sailed on the Richmond, Captain Dunbar) He was granted a manor of 4000 acres there by the Proprietors. [SPAWI.1679.930/1149/1167/1233]

GUERARD, JOHN, councillor of South Carolina, 1758. [JCTP.1758.380/392]

GUERCULT, CHARLES, master of La Francoise captured when bound from Newfoundland to France, 1744. [NA.HCA32.111/1]

GUERIN, ESTIENNE, French refugee, landed in Virginia, 1700. [SPAWI.1700.681]

GUIBALL, JAMES, a French Protestant, petitioned to be shipped to America, possibly went to Jamaica, 1682. [SPAWI.1682.883]

The French in the Americas, 1620-1820

GUICHARD, FRANCIS, and other children of Francis Guichard, French Protestants in St Kitts, a petition, 1714, 1715. [SPAWI.1714.74][JCTP.1715.17]

GUICHARD, FRANCIS, and other children of Arouet Guichard, Huguenots in St Kitts, 1714. [SPAWI.1714.74]

GUICHARD, FRANCIS, a French minister in Charleston, South Carolina, 1732. [FPA#143]

GUICHE, JEAN, wife and three children, French refugees, landed in Virginia, 1700. [SPAWI.1700.681]

GUICHINOT, HENRY, in Antigua, 1723. [APCCol.1725.87]

GUIGNARD, MATHURIN, in Nevis, formerly on St Kitts, 1719. [SPAWI.1719..466i]

GUILLARIE, ..., master of the 250 ton French snow Bon Rencontre captured on 22 March 1757, condemned by the Admiralty Court of New York by 1765. [APCCol.1765.591]

GUILLET, JEAN, master of the La Petite de la Rochelle from Bordeaux to Quebec in 1683. [Gironde Archives, 6B289]; master of Le Marechal de la Rochelle from La Rochelle to Quebec and the West Indies in 1688. [BN.ms11335.194]

GUILLON, J., master of La Flute Royale de Brouage from La Rochelle to Quebec in 1662. [La Rochelle Library, Moreau]

GUILLONNEAU, JEAN, master of the L'Armes d'Amsterdam from La Rochelle to Quebec in 1657. [La Rochelle Municipal Library ms]; master of Le Plaisir de la Rochelle from La Rochelle to Acadia in 1661. [La Rochelle Archives, Moreau, 27]

GUINEAUDEAU, FRANCOIS, born 1714, a weaver, bound from London to Jamaica as an indentured servant, 1736. [CLRO]

GUITTEAU, ..., in St Kitts, 1689, 1690, in Martinique, 1692. [SPAWI.1689.193; 1690.789i/988/1004i; 1692.1993]

GUYHARD, FRANCIS, in St Kitts, 1714. [APCCol.1714.1069]

The French in the Americas, 1620-1820

HAIMS, ..., at Orange, Canada, 1667. [CSPC.1667.1572]

HARDORINE, JAMES, master of the Fortune of Dunkirk bound from Marie Galante but seized by the English of Montserrat, in May 1735. [SPAWI.1736.435]

HAREMBOURG, JEAN, a merchant at Canso, Canada, 1719, 1720. [SPAWI.1719.208ii; 1720.241v]

HARISTOY, JEAN, from Bayonne, master of the St Francois de Guadaloupe captured by an English pirate in July 1723. [SPAWI.1723.416]

HELOT, EDMUND, died on St Kitts in 1680. [SPAWI.1718.510]

HELPTADS, GASPURD, was granted lot 254 in Purrysburgh, Granville County, South Carolina, 1738. [NA.CO5.398]

HENTEYNE, ANTHONY, in Antigua, 1709. [SPAWI.1709.487ii]

HERBOUIN, Captain, master of La Royale, 60 tons, from St Kitts to France in 1681. [SPAWI.1681.236]

HERMITE, ..., a Major at Placentia, Acadia, 1713. [SPAWI.1713.522]

HEUDE, GERARD, in St Vincent, 1773. [JCTP.1773.334]

HEUDE, MICHEL, in St Vincent, 1773. [JCTP.1773.334]

HINSELIN, ..., in Guadaloupe, 1674. [SPAWI.1674.1333]

HIRIART, PIERRE, master of the L'Americain captured when bound for the West Indies in 1748. [NA.HCA32.95/2]

HIRIGOYAN, GERARD, master of Le Cezar which was captured when bound for the West Indies in 1748. [NA.HCA32.102/1]

HOCQUART, ..., claim to lands on the lower part of the River St Lawrence in 1763, and on Lake Champlain and at Gros Mecatinat, New York, 1772. [JCTP.1763.406; 1772.317]

HONORATI, JEAN, master of Le Vanqueur which was captured when bound from the West Indies in 1747. [NA.HCA32.157/1]

The French in the Americas, 1620-1820

HOSIER, Captain, at St Jago de la Vega, 1712. [SPAWI.1712.148v

HUGUET, JULIEN, master of Le George which was captured when bound from the West Indies in 1747. [NA.HCA32.114]

HUGUIN, DAVID, was granted 100 acres in Granville County, South Carolina, 1738. [NA.CO5.398][SPAWI.1738.281]

HURLER, GABRIEL, French refugees, landed in Virginia, 1700. [SPAWI.1700.681]

HURTAIN, JACQUES, master of the Clerbault from La Rochelle to Acadia and Quebec in 1667. [La Rochelle Archives]

HURTIN, GUILLAUME, master of Marguerite de Brouage, from France to Acadia in 1661. [La Rochelle Library, Moreau, 64]

IMBERT, JEAN, and wife, French refugees, landed in Virginia, 1700. [SPAWI.1700.681]

INGLERINE, ANNA, was granted 250 acres in Granville County, South Carolina, 1738. [NA.CO5.398]

JAMIN, PIERRE, master of Moise de la Rochelle from La Rochelle to Acadia in 1658. [La Rochelle Archives, Savin ms; Teuleron ms]

JANSON, JAN, master of the 200 ton ship Chasseur, of the Royal West India Company of France, built at Honfleur, captured by the Dutch en route from St Kitts to France, 1673. [SPAWI.1673.1056]

JA'TRUE, ..., on St Vincent. 1730. [SPAWI.1730.260iii]

JAVELLEAU, JEAN, master of Le Sauvage de Bordeaux from Bordeaux to Canada in 1686. [Bordeaux Archives, Ferrand]

JEAFFARD, JEAN, in St Kitts, 1672, 1680. [SPAWI.1672.903; 1680.1312]

JENTEL, JACQUES, master of Le Diamont de Bordeaux from France to Canada in 1690. [Gironde Archives, 6B74.48, B295]

JEUNKER, ..., an interpreter from Canada, at Onnondage, New York, 1709. [JCTP.1711.834i]

The French in the Americas, 1620-1820

JOHANNOT, DANIEL, a distiller in Boston, 1720. [SPAWI.1720.22i]

JOLIET, LOUIS, was granted the Mingan Islands, Labrador, 1764. [JCTP.1763.382; 1764.452]

JOLY, LOUIS, master of Les Trois Amis which was captured when bound from the West Indies in 1744. [NA.HCA32.155]

JOLY, PIERRE, master of L'Henriette which was captured when bound from the West Indies in 1747. [NA.HCA32.117]

JONCURE, ..., a French interpreter among the Indians of the Five Nations, 1719. [SPAWI.1720.48]

JOUANNY, JEAN, wife and two children, French refugees, landed in Virginia, 1700. [SPAWI.1700.681]

JOUBERT, ..., a French Catholic in St Kitts, 1686. [APCCol.1715.1225]

JOURDAIN, FRANCIS, born 1695, a joiner, bound from London to Maryland as an indentured servant 1725. [CLRO]

JOURDAN, PIERRE, in Dominica, 1771. [JCTP.1773.274]

JOURDON, MARIE, French refugees, landed in Virginia, 1700. [SPAWI.1700.681]

JOURDON, SIMON, French refugees, landed in Virginia, 1700. [SPAWI.1700.681]

JOVENNE, PIERRE, master of the La Fidele which was captured when bound from the West Indies in 1746. [NA.HCA32.111/1]

JULIE, ROSE, in Dominica, 1771. [JCTP.1773.248]

JUSTINIEN, Father, a priest in Nova Scotia, 1720. [SPAWI.1720.180xvi/241ix]

L'ABBE, FRANCOIS, master of La Parfaitte which was captured when bound from the West Indies in 1747. [NA.HCA32.147/1]

LA BARETT, ..., a naval commander in the West Indies, 1670. [SPAWI.1671.508]

The French in the Americas, 1620-1820

LA BAT, Pere, in French West Indies, 1734. [SPAWI.1735.602i]

LA BAT, PIERRE DENIS, master of La Jeune Janette which was captured when bound for the West Indies in 1745. [NA.HCA32.118/2]

LA BETEUX, Mrs, at Samuel Francis's tavern, Dock Street, New York, 1783. [HMC. American.iv.49]

LA BLANC, JOSEPH, in Beau-Bassin, Nova Scotia, later in South Carolina, 1756. [JCTP.1756.226]

LA CHANEY, ..., a merchant in Canada, 1682. [SPAWI.1699.266]

LA COUR, PIERRE, French refugees, landed in Virginia, 1700. [SPAWI.1700.681]

LA COUSAY, PH., a planter on Nevis, 1712. [JCTP]

LA DOUCEUR, ..., a soldier, killed by the Chicachas at Fort Saint Claude in 1730. [HLF]

LA FACE, L e Sieur, an army officer captive in Virginia, 1755. [HLF]

LA FAILLE, JEAN BAPTISTE, in Dominica, 1771. [JCTP.1773.274]

LA FERTEY, SAMUEL PICART, in Antigua, 1709. [SPAWI.1709.487ii]

LA FFITTE, PETER, was granted 450 acres in Granville County, South Carolina, 1738. [NA.CO5.398]

LAFFON, ..., a planter in Capisterre Quarter, St Kitts, before 1717. [JCTP.1717.261]

LA FLAMME, ..., a soldier, killed by the Chicachas at Fort Saint Claude in 1730. [HLF]

LA FOND, LEONARD, in Dominica, 1772. [JCTP.1772.319]

LA FONTAINE, ..., in Great Mekatinat, Quebec, claimed islands of Mingan and Anticosti, 1764. [JCTP.71.449/452]

LA FORTUNE, ..., in St Kitts, 1672. [SPAWI.1672.903]

The French in the Americas, 1620-1820

LA FORTUNE, ..., a soldier, killed by the Chicachas at Fort Saint Claude in 1730. [HLF]

LA FOSSE, ..., in Acadia, 1715. [SPAWI.1715.568xiA]

LA GARS, PIERRE, master of L'Intrepide which was captured when bound from the West Indies in 1744. [NA.HCA32.118/1]

LA GERE, JOSEPH, master of La Fidele which was captured when bound from the West Indies in 1744. [NA.HCA32.111/1]

LA GRANGE, BARNARDUS, a Loyalist in New York, 1783. [HMC.IV.107/268]

LA GUARD, ..., residing at Buck Row, Virginia, 1624.

LA GUARIGNE, ..., in St Kitts, 1674. [SPAWI.1674.1273]

LA GRANADE, JACQUES, of the schooner Romaine de Martinique, at Barbados, 1725. [SPAWI.1725.398]

LA GRANGE, C., in Dominica, 1771. [JCTP.1773.274]

LA GRANGE, Captain, master of La Veste from La Rochelle to Quebec in 1696. [La Rochelle Archives, Gariteau]

LA GUARIGNE, ..., in St Kitts, 1673. [SPAWI.1674.1273]

LA HAY, ..., a French privateer at St Augustine, 1720. [SPAWI.1720.516]

LA JOYE, ..., a soldier, killed by the Chicachas at Fort Saint Claude in 1730. [HLF]

LALANDE, JACQUES, was granted the Island of Mingan on 10 March 1679, also Anticosti Island in 1680. [JCTP.71.452/453]

LA LESSE, BENJAMIN, master of the L'Aimable Susanne captured when bound from Louisburg to France in 1745. [NA.HCA32.95/1]

LA LONGUE, ..., in Quebec, 1723. [SPAWI.1723.805]

LAMANDE, FRANCIS, interpreter aboard the Two Friends of Boston from Boston to Cape Francois and return via Charleston, South Carolina, 1723. [SPAWI.1724.85ii]

The French in the Americas, 1620-1820

LA MARQUE, ANTOINE, master of Le Petit Fonds which was captured when bound from the West Indies in 1747. [NA.HCA32.143/1]

LAMBERT, HENRY, a woollen draper, with his wife, to emigrate to Virginia, 1621. [CSPC.Addenda; Colonial Correspondence, Vol.i,#45]

LAMBERT, Captain, a French planter in St Kitts before 1717. [JCTP.1717.261]

LANBANY, ..., of la Sarre, a French soldier captured in Canada, 1759. [SM.21.541]

LANCIEUX, GODEFROY, master of La Ville de St Malo which was captured when bound from the West Indies in 1747. [NA.HCA32.156/1]

LANDRY, CHARLES, at River, Nova Scotia, 1727. [SPAWI.1727.789]

LANGELIER, JOHN, a planter in Antigua, 1718. [SPAWI.1718.413]

LANGEVIN, HENRI, master of Le Nicolas de St Gilles from La Rochelle to Acadia in 1636. [Charente Maritime Archives, Teuleron charter]

L'ANGLOIS, LOUIS, in Dominica, dead by 1772. [JCTP.1772.319]

LANGUEMAR, NICHOLAS, land grant in Carolina, 1685. [SPAWI,1685.250]

LANGUILE,......., in Canada, 1723. [SPAWI.1723.805]

LANQUIN, Captain, master of Le Vollantiere at Martinique, 1702.

LANSWINE, ..., in St Kitts, 1672. [SPAWI.1672.903]

LANVEAUX, JEAN, a prisoner of the English in Newfoundland, 1704. [SPAWI.1704.315i]

LA PARE, Madam, at Fort ....., Quebec, 1711. [JCTP.1711.673]

LA PIERRE, JOHN, a minister on Cape Fear, North Carolina, 1732. [FPA#90]

LA PLACE, ..., and Company, merchants in St Domingo, 1760. [JCTP.1763.386]

LA POTERIE, B., in Guadaloupe, a letter, 1681. [SPAWI.1681.190]

LA PRADELLE, Colonel JEAN, in St Kitts, 1726. [SPAWI.1726.236]

The French in the Americas, 1620-1820

LA RALDI, DOMINIC, a merchant at Cape Francis in America, partner of John Blancau a merchant in Bordeaux, France, deceased, late husband of Margaret Renaire, an appeal in Jamaica re the sale of the <u>Santa Rosa</u> and her cargo, 1756. [APCCol.1756.275]

LA RANDA, Madam, in Shamblin, Quebec, 1711. [JCTP.1711.673]

LA RICHARDIERNE, ..., a prisoner of the English in Newfoundland, 1703. [SPAWI.1704.315h/i]

LARMOIGNEUX, ..., in Martinique, 1683. [SPAWI.1683.871xi]

LA ROCHE, JEAN BAPTISTE, in Dominica, 1772. [JCTP.1772.319]

LA ROCHE, WILLIAM, in Dominica, 1772. [JCTP.1772.319]

LARON, ..., a chart-maker at New York, 1733. [SPAWI.1733.441]

LA RONDE, ..., at the capture of St John's, Newfoundland, 1709; was granted Cape Sables by the French king by 1713. [SPAWI.1709.890ii; 1713.522]

LAROUX, ..., master of a merchant vessel trading from Martinique, 1704. [SPAWI.1704.420]

LA ROUX, MICHEL, master of <u>La Francoise</u> which was captured when bound from Newfoundland in 1744. [NA.HCA32.111/1]

L'ARTIQUE, JEAN JACQUES, a prisoner in Guadaloupe, 1761. [Cal.H.O.pp.1761/306]

LA SALLE, ..., in Canada, pre 1681. [SPAWI.1681.874]

LASCAL, JEAN, a seaman aboard a fishing boat, captured at St Pierre, Newfoundland, a prisoner of war in Greenlaw, Scotland, died there 13 July 1806. [NA.ADM.103.155/199, 103.624]

LASERRE, ANTOINE, in Dominica, 1772. [JCTP.1773.280]

LASSERRE, PIERRE, master of <u>L'Heureux St Pierre</u> which was captured when bound from Martinique in 1747. [NA.HCA32.117]

LA SHAS, Pere, a Jesuit priest in Nova Scotia, 1711. [JCTP.1711.673]

LA SONDE, BERNARD, a merchant at Canso, Canada, 1719. [SPAWI.1719.208ii/213i]

LASSONDE, ..., a French pilot aboard a sloop bound from New England to Louisbourg, 1720. [SPAWI.1720.241.vii]

LA TANNEE, ..., French minister at Rappahannock, Virginia, 1701. [SPAWI.1701.719]

LA TOUR, ..., a French officer, with his wife, in Boston, New England, 1714. [SPAWI.1715.568iii]

LA TOUR, ..., in Nova Scotia before 1734. [SPAWI.1734.454][JCTP.1732.300]

LAURET, PIERRE, French refugee, landed in Virginia, 1700. [SPAWI.1700.681]

LA VALLIERE, ..., Governor of Acadia, at Port Royal, 1684. [SPAWI.1684.1863iv]

LA VARENNE, ..., General of the French Islands, 1717. [JCTP.1717,245]

LA VAUX, Captain ALEXANDER, an engineer in St Kitts, possibly a French spy, 1742. [APCCol.1742.529]

LA VERDAINT, NICHOLAS, and his wife Theodora, in Dominica, 1776. [JCTP.Vol.83.13]

LA VICOUNTT, JOHN, a planter in Antigua, 1718. [SPAWI.1718.729]

LA VIVON, ..., master of Le Cour Volant de La Rochelle, a pirate, at Isle de Vacour, Hispaniola, 1669; at Port Royal, Jamaica, 1673. [SPAWI.1669.1207; 1673.21]

LAYNARD, JOHN, from France, an indentured servant bound from London to Barbados aboard the Hopewell in 1683. [CLRO]

LAZOUE, ..., commander of the sloop Sainte Elizabeth, bound from Fort Louis, with a company of Swiss troops, bound for Mississippi, which mutinied and landed at Charleston, South Carolina, 1722. [SPAWI.1722.372iii]

LE BAILLI DE SOUVRAY, ..., purchased St Croix from the Compagnie de St Christopher et Santa Cruz in 1651. [SPAWI.1734.388ii]

The French in the Americas, 1620-1820

LE BARONE, ... in St Kitts, 1672. [SPAWI.1672.903]

LE BAS, JAMES, a Huguenot, master of the Elizabeth of Dieppe, was captured by the English on his way home from the French Plantations and Barbados in 1654. [CSPC.XII.28/29]

LE BAS, JAMES, was granted land in Carolina, 1685, also in 1689. [SPAWI.1685.373; 1689.653]

LE BAS, JAMES, was granted 200 acres in Berkley County, South Carolina, 1737. [NA.CO5.398]

LE BAS, PAUL PIERRE, in South Carolina, 1716. [SPAWI.1716.407i]

LE BEAUF, JEROME, was granted 500 acres in Berkley County, South Carolina, 1738. [NA.CO5.398]

LE BLANC, PIERRE, a farmer in Nova Scotia, 1714. [JCTP.1714.5]

LE BLANC, RENE, at Grand Pre, Les Menis #9, St John's River, Bay of Fundy, 1732. [SPAWI.1732.259][JCTP.1732.321]

LE BOONE, JACQUE, in St Kitts, 1672. [SPAWI.1672.903]

LE BORGNE, Sieur DE BELLE ISLE, ALEXANDER, in Annapolis Royal, Nova Scotia, 1734. [SPAWI.1734.164i]

LE BORGNE, Sieur DE BELLE ISLE, ..., Governor of Acadia in 1657, at Port Royal, 1668. [SPAWI.1667.1600][CSPC.1668.1898]

LE BOUR, LEW, master of the 6 gun pirate ship *Blanco* captured off Barbados, 1718. [SPAWI.1718.742]

LE BOUTEAUX, GABRIEL, in New York, 1695. [SPAWI.1695.1646]

LE BRETON, JOHN, petitioned for land in Nova Scotia, 1767. [JCTP.74.182]

LE BRETON, Captain NICHOLAS, a French shipmaster from Montserrat to Galway, Ireland, 1654. [CSPC.XII.25][NA.COl.XII.25]

LE BRETON, PIERRE, master of Saint Pierre de Bordeaux from Bordeaux to Quebec and the West Indies in 1684, and from Bordeaux to Quebec in 1685.

The French in the Americas, 1620-1820

[Gironde Archives, 6B70/118, 6B71/170, 6B290; Bordeaux Archives, Ferrand.103]

LE BOUE, RENOLD, in Cape Breton, 1720. [SPAWI.1720.241ii]

LE BRUNANT, JOSEPH BONNAVANTURE, master of Le Triomphant which was captured when bound for the West Indies in 1748. [NA.HCA32.155]

LECA, JAN, a Walloon, a laborer, with his wife and five children, to emigrate to Virginia, 1621. [CSPC.Addenda; Colonial Correspondence, Vol.i,#45]

LE CEGUILLO, Captain, master of L'Invincible at Martinique, 1702. [SPAWI.1702.195]

LE CERF, NICHOLAS JACQUES, master of the privateer La Necessaire which was captured when bound for the West Indies in 1747. [NA.HCA32.139]

LE CHAISE, Father, in Acadia, 1721. [SPAWI.1721.743]

LE CHEVALIER, JEAN, a joiner at Fort Albany, New York, 1701. [SPAWI.1701.584]

LE CHOLET, ..., in St Domingo, a letter, 1749. [JCTP.1750.49]

LE CLERC, CLAUDE, master of L'Estoile du Jour from France to Quebec in 1695. [Charente Maritime Archives.B235.336]

LE COINTRE, JEAN BAPTISTE, in Dominica, 1772. [JCTP.1773.280]

LE COMPT, JOHN, in Dorchester County, Maryland, 1701. [SPAWI.1701.425]

LE CORDIER, Captain, master of the 180 ton ship St Etienne bound from France via Madeira and Guinea to the French West Indies, was seized by the English in the River Serbonne, Guinea, in August 1672. [SPAWI.1673.1111]

LE CRAS, Captain, captured the sloop London in Bay Verte in August 1750. [JCTP.1750.96]

LE CRAVEREN, FRANCOIS, master of Le Pont Carre which was captured when bound from the West Indies in 1747. [NA.HCA32.147/1]

LE CROC, ... in St Kitts, 1672. [SPAWI.1672.903]

The French in the Americas, 1620-1820

LE CURIEUX, JACQUES, in Martinique licensed to hunt, fish, and cut wood on St Lucia by the Governor of Martinique, 1688. [SPAWI.1688.1718.i]

LE DEPENSIER, JEAN, master of Le Fort de Nantes a privateer, which was captured bound from the West Indies in 1746. [NA.HCA32.111/4-7]

LE DUFF, MARIET, in St Pierre, Martinique, legatee of Samuel Cunningham, 1796. [PRONI.D1108/A9]

LE DUKE, JACOBUS, gunner of Plymouth Fort, Montserrat, 1694. [SPAWI.1694.802]

LE FEBURE, JEAN BAPTISTE, in Dominica, 1775. [JCTP.1775.441]

LE FEVRE, HIPPOLIT, in New Jersey, 1678. [SPAWI.1678.778]

LE FONDS, ..., an alleged illegal trader on Cape Breton, 1728. [SPAWI.1729.790]

LE GAIVE, ... an officer at Cape Breton, 1733. [SPAWI.1733.440]

LE GARDEUR, ..., a French merchant in, or trading with, Jamaica, 1719. [SPAWI.1719.167i]

LE GAY, ISAAC, in Barbados, 1729. [APCCol.1730.225]

LE GEAN, PONTUS, a bolting cloth weaver, with his wife and three children, to emigrate to Virginia, 1621. [CSPC.Addenda; Colonial Correspondence, Vol.i,#45]

LE GENTIL, LOUIS, master of the L'Alcion captured when bound for the West Indies in 1745. [NA.HCA32.96/1]

LE GONARD DE SOURDEVAL, SEBASTIEN, Commandant of St Pierre and Miquelon, 1702 to 1709.

LE GRAND, ISAAC, Sieur d'ANARVILLE, land grant in Carolina, 1686. [SPAWI.1686.833]

LE GRAND, ..., Commandant of Dominica, 1736. [SPAWI.1736.361]

The French in the Americas, 1620-1820

LE GRANDE, ..., a planter in Capisterre Quarter, St Kitts, before 1717. [JCTP.1717.261]

LE GREE, ..., in St Kitts, 1672. [SPAWI.1672.903]

LE GUEROULT DE LA PLACE, JACQUES PIERRE, master of L'Intrepide which was captured when bound from the West Indies in 1746. [NA.HCA32.118/1]

LE JAN, FRANCIS, was granted 33 acres in Berkley County, South Carolina, 1738. [NA.CO5.398]

LE JAY, ISAAC, land grant in Carolina, 1685. [SPAWI.1686.133]

LE JEU, FRANCIS, a minister St James', Goose Creek, South Carolina, 1712.

LE JEUNE, GREGOIRE, a shoemaker, with his wife and four children, to emigrate to Virginia, 1621. [CSPC.Addenda; Colonial Correspondence, Vol.i,#45]

LE JEUNE, ..., in Grenada, 1768. [CalHOP.1768/832/945/955]

LE LOUTRE, ..., a missionary priest at Chiconecto, Nova Scotia, 1749. [JCTP.1750.65]

LE MANCHAN, Captain, master of Le Constant at Martinique in 1702. [SPAWI.1702.195]

LE MANDE, FRANCIS, in Carolina, 1724. [JCTP.1724.128]

LE MERCIER, ANDREW, pastor of the French church in Boston, proposed to establish a colony of French Protestants in Nova Scotia, 1729; petitioned to settle on Isle du Sables, 1738. [SPAWI.1729.917III/994; 1738.138]

LE MERKIN, WILLIAM, at Portugal Cove, Newfoundland, 1731. [SPAWI.1731.422]

LE MESURER, GUILLAUME, master of the Deux Souers et Marie from Newfoundland to Bilbao, Spain, pre 1717. [SPAWI.1717.493]

LE MOINE, JEAN, a deserter from Placentia, Newfoundland, 1704. [JCTP.1704.66]

The French in the Americas, 1620-1820

LE MOTE, …., in St Kitts, 1672. [SPAWI.1672.903]

LE MOYNE, JAMES, land grant in Carolina, 1686. [SPAWI.1686.833]

LE MOYNE, PIERRE, master of <u>Saint Jean de Dieppe</u> from France to Quebec in 1664. [La Rochelle Archives, Cherbonnier]

LE MOYNE D'IBERVILLE, PIERRE, Governor of Louisiana, 1699. [HLF]

LE MOYNE DE BIENVILLE, JOSEPH, Governor of Louisiana, 1702, 1708. [HLF]

L'ENCLUME, …….., a soldier, killed by the Chicachas at Fort Saint Claude in 1730. [HLF]

LE NORMANT, ……, intendant at Louisbourg, 1733. [SPAWI.1733.439]

LE NOVINAN, ………, at Cape Breton, 1733. [SPAWI.1733.140]

LE PAGE, ……, in St Domingo, 1689. [SPAWI.1689.52i]

LE PONT, ……, at Quebec, 1629. [CSPC.V.16]

LE REAUX, JOHN, a French Protestant, naturalised in New York in 1692, master of a sloop which he sunk and absconded with money, caught and imprisoned in Boston, he escaped via Canada to France, from La Rochelle aboard a bark to New England, captured an imprisoned in New York in 1693, acquitted in 1695. [SPAWI.1693.612/711/783/804/952/1356/1998]

LE ROU, JAN, a Walloon printer, with his wife and six children, to emigrate to Virginia, 1621. [CSPC.Addenda; Colonial Correspondence, Vol.i,#45]

LE ROUX, BARTHOLEMEW, a land grant in Carolina, 1683. [SPAWI.1683.1268]

LE ROUX, BARTHOLEMEW, in New York, 1689. [SPAWI.1689.458]

LE ROUX, JACOB, in Antigua, a deposition, 1710. [JCTP.1710.324vii] [SPAWI.1710.324vii]

LE ROUX, MICHEL, master of <u>La Francoise</u> captured when bound from Newfoundland to France in 1747. [NA.HCA32.111/1]

LE ROUX, PETER, died in Virginia, probate 1654, Prerogative Court of Canterbury

The French in the Americas, 1620-1820

LE ROY, ANTHONY, master of the Mareschal d'Asfeldt bound from St Domingo to Nantz, France, in 1735. [SPAWI.1735.152]

LE ROY, ETIENNE, master of the St Rene de Pornie, fishing on the Banks of Newfoundland, 1723. [SPAWI.1723.758ii]

LE ROY, JEROME, a cloth weaver, with his wife and four children, to emigrate to Virginia, 1621. [CSPC.Addenda; Colonial Correspondence, Vol.i,#45]

LE SAGE, FRANCOIS, a pirate, 1684. [SPAWI.1684.1839]

LES BOURG, ..., a French inhabitant of Les Mines, Nova Scotia, a letter, 3 October 1720. [SPAWI.1720.241xv]

L'ESCOTT, FRANCES, a widow in Charleston, South Carolina, will/administration, 1753, Prerogative Court of Canterbury.

LESNARD, JEAN, a French refugee, landed in Virginia, 1700. [SPAWI.1700.681]

LESPINARD, ANTONIE, letter, 1686; from Canada to Albany, New York, 1687. [SPAWI.1686.969; 1687.1421]

LE SUEUR, LEONARD, in Dominica, 1771. [JCTP.1773.274]

LE TOREY, HENRY, master of Le Solide, a Newfoundland fisheries ship, which was captured in 1744. [NA.HCA32.151/1]

LEUADOU, JEAN, and wife, French refugees, landed in Virginia, 1700. [SPAWI.1700.681]

LEUESQZ, MARIE, a French refugee, landed in Virginia, 1700. [SPAWI.1700.681]

LEUSIER, MICHEL, a cloth weaver, with his wife and child, to emigrate to Virginia, 1621. [CSPC.Addenda; Colonial Correspondence, Vol.i,#45]

LE VANIER, LOUIS, born 1701, a book-keeper from Calais, an indentured servant bound from London to Barbados in 1718. [CLRO]

LE VASSEUR, ANTOINE, master of Les Deux Freres which was captured when bound from the West Indies in 1744. [NA.HCA32.104/1]

LE VILLIER, ..., in St Kitts, 1672. [SPAWI.1672.903]

The French in the Americas, 1620-1820

LEWREAU, MOYSE, a French refugee, landed in Virginia, 1700. [SPAWI.1700.681]

L'FAVOUR, ..., in Quebec, 1711. [JCTP.1711.673]

LION, JEAN JACQUES, in Dominica, 1771. [JCTP.1773.248]

LONGVILLE, ..., petitioned for a settlement for French Protestants in North America, 20 May 1717. [JCTP.1717.233]

LOOBY, BAPTISTE, Justice of the Court of Common Pleas in the Virgin Islands, 1778. [JCTP.Vol.85.149]

LOREINE, ..., in St Kitts, 1672. [SPAWI.1672.903]

LOTBINIERE, ..., land grant at Lakes Champlain and St Sacrament, New York, 1764, 1772. [JCTP.71.218/222]

LOYARD, Father JEAN, a Jesuit missionary on the River St John, Acadia, 1715, 1718. [SPAWI.1715.142iv/658; 1718.789]

LUBIN, CHARLES, master of La Belle Manon which was captured when bound for the West Indies in 1747. [NA.HCA32.99/1]

MACHEE, PETER, born in France during 1671, a mariner who settled in New York in 1692, master of the Batchelor's Endeavour which was captured by a French privateer on 1 May 1697 and taken to Martinique. [NA.HCA. Thomas Dubois versus Andrew Way, 1698]

MACHIER, CHARLES HENRY, a fish merchant in Placentia, Newfoundland, 1715. [SPAWI.1715.123]

MAFFIER, PIERRE, master of Le Diamant which was captured when bound for the West Indies in 1748. [NA.HCA32.104/2]

MAGESCAZ, JEAN, master of Le Bon, which was captured when bound for the West Indies in 1746. [NA.HCA32.99/2]

MAHEUT, LOUIS, master of the L'Archange Saint Michel de Amsterdam from France to Acadia in 1680. [La Rochelle Municipal Library ms]

The French in the Americas, 1620-1820

MAILLARD, MARY, a French Protestant in St Kitts, 1712, 1714, 1715. [APCCol.1714.1069] [JCTP.1712.395;1715.17]

MAJEAU, PETER, a planter in St Mary's parish, Jamaica, father of Thomas and Elizabeth, an Act, 1751. [JCTP.1755.190]

MALLEFAUT, CLAUD, a French refugee, landed in Virginia, 1700. [SPAWI.1700.681]

MALLEFAUT, JEAN, with his mother, French refugees, landed in Virginia, 1700. [SPAWI.1700.681]

MALLET, PIERRE, a French refugee, landed in Virginia, 1700. [SPAWI.1700.681]

MANDRET, JACQUES, from Sabel D'Olone, France, bound for Newfoundland aboard the St Anna, master Jacques Fevre, 1640. [GAR.ONA.169.78.123]

MANGEANT, Sieur, a French gentleman in Nova Scotia, 1729. [SPAWI.1729.789]

MANGER, JAMES, born in Havre de Grace, France, seaman aboard the Anne and Katherine of New York, from New York to Maryland bound for London in 1690. [NA.HCA.Rex v. The Anne and Katherine, 1692]

MANIGAULT, GABRIEL, was granted 1000 acres on the Peedee River, South Carolina, 1738. [NA.CO5.398]

MANJEAN, ..., an alleged murderer, fled from Canada to Nova Scotia, taken to England in 1730. [SPAWI.1730.411]

MARCHAIS, JEAN, master of La Diligente which was captured when bound from the West Indies in 1747. [NA.HCA32.105]

MARCHIS, JAMES, was granted 250 acres in Granville County, South Carolina, 1738. [NA.CO5.398]

MARESCHALL, ..., a planter at Pensez y Bien, and a property owner in Basse Terre, St Kitts, before 1717. [JCTP.1717.261]

MAREST DE LA TOUR, ..., an army officer with 23 years service in Louisiana by 1759. [Archive des Colonies, serie D, troupes colonials, registres D 2C.50/58]

The French in the Americas, 1620-1820

MARIECOUR,........, in Canada, 1699. [SPAWI.1699.878vi]

MARIN, PIERRE PAUL, Captain of Fort Presqu'ile, Ohio, 1752. [HLF]

MARKLEY, JAMES, born 1662, son of James Markley of Ayre, France, bound for Maryland aboard the Assistance in 1684. [CLRO]

MAROHE, JEAN, a French refugee, landed in Virginia, 1700. [SPAWI.1700.681]

MAROT, YVES, master of Le Vainqueur de la Rochelle from La Rochelle to Quebec and the West Indies, 1697. [Charente Maritime Archives, B5693]

MARTAIN, MATTHEW, land grant at Cobaquid, Nova Scotia, dead by 1734. [SPAWI.1732.259;1734.454]

MARTEILHE, JOHN, a merchant in Quebec, 1764. [JCTP.1764.254]

MARTELL, MAGDALAINE, a French refugee, landed in Virginia, 1700. [SPAWI.1700.681]

MARTIN, ANTOINE, with his wife and child, to emigrate to Virginia, 1621. [CSPC.Addenda; Colonial Correspondence, Vol.i,#45]

MARTIN, CHARLES, in Dominica, 1772. [JCTP.1772.319]

MARTIN, JAMES, was granted 800 acres in Craven County, South Carolina, 1737. [NA.CO5.398]

MARTIN, JEAN, a resident of New Brunswick, 1786. [NA.AO13.80.325]

MARTIN, JEANNE, a young girl, to emigrate to Virginia, 1621. [CSPC.Addenda; Colonial Correspondence, Vol.i,#45]

MARTIN, MATIEU, master of the Conpuis de la Rochelle from France to Quebec in 1696. [Charente Maritime Archives, B5292]

MARTIN, MATTHEW, seignieur of Cobequit, Nova Scotia, 1732. [JCTP.1732.321]

MARTIN, SIMON, a resident of New Brunswick, 1786. [NA.AO13.80.325]

MASSEY, PHILIP, was granted 500 acres in Craven County, South Carolina, 1737. [NA.CO5.398]

MASSON, JEAN, master of Esperance from La Rochelle to Quebec in 1669; master of La Diane from France to Quebec in 1675. [Charente Maritime ms.B5669-5674]

MASSON, MARY, was granted 100 acres in Granville County, South Carolina, 1738. [NA.CO5.398]

MASSONEAU, RENE, a French refugee, landed in Virginia, 1700. [SPAWI.1700.681]

MASSY, ..., captain of a French ship that attacked the Canso settlement in Nova Scotia, 1720; 1722. [SPAWI.1720.241ii; 1722.234viiiC]

MATHEY, ABRAHAM, was granted 200 acres in Granville County, South Carolina, 1738. [NA.CO5.398]

MATON, PHILIPPE, a vine-dresser, with his wife, five children, and two servants, to emigrate to Virginia, 1621. [CSPC.Addenda; Colonial Correspondence, Vol.i,#45]

MATTON, ANTHONIE, and wife, French refugees, landed in Virginia, 1700. [SPAWI.1700.681]

MAULION, LUCY, widow of Jean Maulion, in St Vincent, 1772. [JCTP.1772.319]

MAURIE, JAMES, son of a French immigrant, educated at the College of William and Mary, applied to become an Anglican clergyman in Virginia, 1741. [FPA#192]

MEE, NICHOLAS ELIE, master of La Basile captured when bound for the West Indies in 1747. [NA.HCA32.99/1]

MELANSON, CLAUD, at Cape Bellair, Nova Scotia, 1734. [SPAWI.1734.164i]

MENAGER, JEAN, a French refugee, landed in Virginia, 1700. [SPAWI.1700.681]

MERAE, JOHN, an Anglican minister in St Kitts, 1732. [FPA#279]

MERCIER, BARTHOLEMEW, in the Bahamas, 1699. [SPAWI.1699.385]

MERRET, DANIEL, was granted 50 acres in Granville County, South Carolina, 1738. [NA.CO5.398]

The French in the Americas, 1620-1820

MERRET, JOHN DANIEL, was granted 150 acres in Granville County, South Carolina, 1738. [NA.CO5.398]

MEUNIER, FRANCIS, a Huguenot in the French sector of St Kitts who was forced to abandon his plantation, father of Mary widow of Peter Maillard, and Arouet wife of .... Guychard, a petition, 1714. [SPAWI.1714.74/327]

MEURE, ..., a French Protestant in St Kitts, 1716. [JCTP.1716.197]

MEYER, HENRY, a merchant planter in Antigua, denizised 1675. [SPAWI.1675.376]

MICHAEL, LEWIS, was granted 50 acres in Granville County, South Carolina, 1738. [NA.CO5.398]

MICHEL, ..., master of the La Sara de Rochelle in the West Indies, 1680; a privateer in the Caribbean Sea, 1685. [SPAWI.1680.1437; 1685.148/269]

MICHEL, Captain, commander of a French *guardacosta* at Hispaniola, 1738. [SPAWI.1738.417]

MIGUEL, JEAN, master of La Rene Marie which was captured when bound from the West Indies in 1747. [NA.HCA32.149/1]

MIGUEL, RENE, master of the Alexandre de Nantes captured when bound for the West Indies in 1744. [NA.HCA32.96/3]

MINGEON, FRANCOIS CASTAIGNET, master of the L'Aimable Jeanne of Bordeaux captured when bound from the West Indies for France in 1745. [NA.HCA32.94/1]

MILET, PIERRE, a Jesuit among the Oneidas, New York, 1693. [SPAWI.1693.179vii/479/611/829/991/1860IV]

MILLECHAMP, ..., a French minister in Goose Creek, South Carolina, 1732. [FPA#143]

MINEVIELLE, DAVID, in New York, co-owner of the Rhode Island built sloop Good Intent, 1717. [JCTP.1717.437]

MINGOT, ELIZABETH, a French refugee, landed in Virginia, 1700. [SPAWI.1700.681]

MINIEL,......, from France as Governor of Acadia, 1687. [SPAWI.1687.1413[

MINOT, ABRAHAM, a French refugee, landed in Virginia, 1700. [SPAWI.1700.681]

MINVIELE, Colonel GABRIEL, in New York, 1695; in Canada, 1701. [SPAWI.1695.105/1515/1716/1744/1864; 1701.777]

MOLINEUX,......, in Montserrat, 1724. [SPAWI.1724.400]

MONBEUIL, PIERRE, master of La Perroquot de la Rochelle from La Rochelle to Acadia and Quebec in 1680. [Charente Maritime Archives, B5679; Teuleron ms]

MONDAVY, RAYMOND, master of the L'Aimable Martha captured when bound from the West Indies for France in 1747. [NA.HCA32.97/1]

MONDESIR, THURET, on St Vincent, 1764. [JCTP.1764.283]

MONIACK, ..., Governor of Placentia, Newfoundland, 1708. [SPAWI.1708.60]

MONIER, JOHN, in St Johns, Newfoundland, 1730. [SPAWI.1730.503iv]

MONLOUIS, LOUIS MARTIN, in Grenada, 1769. [JCTP.1769.156]

MONOD, GASPAR JOEL, chaplain to the Governor of Guadaloupe, 1759. [FPA#317]

MONTARVILLE, Lieutenant of Marines, Chevalier de St Louis, a French soldier captured in Canada, 1759. [SM.21.541]

MONTGOLFIER, ..., Vicar General of Quebec, a letter, 1761. [JCTP.1763.308]

MONTMILLON, ... an Anglican chaplain in Quebec, 1769. [FPA#9]

MOQUET, FRANCOIS, in Grenada, 1769. [JCTP.1769.156]

MORANDAIS, LOUIS LAMBERT, in Dominica, 1772. [JCTP.1773.280]

MORCHOISNE, JEAN BAPTISTE, master of the L'Aimable Vainqueur captured when bound from the West Indies to France in 1744. [NA.HCA32.97/1]

The French in the Americas, 1620-1820

MOREAU, JEAN, a French refugee, landed in Virginia, 1700. [SPAWI.1700.681]

MOREFLAT,...., in St Kitts, 1672. [SPAWI.1672.903]

MOREL, PIERRE, petitioned for a land grant in Heigeat or Highgate, Georgia, 1737. [NA.CO5.639.145/145D]

MORGAT, JEAN, master of Le Fleur de Mai Chaillevette from La Rochelle to Quebec in 1690. [Charente Maritime Archives, B235]

MORIN, THEOPHILE, a French Protestant, petitioned to be shipped to America, possibly went to Jamaica, 1682. [SPAWI.1682.883]

MORNANT, JEAN BAPTISTE, master of La Notre Dame de Protection from La Rochelle to Canada and Newfoundland in 1690. [Charente Maritime Archives, B5686]

MORRIS, JACOB, born 1670 in France, an indentured servant bound from London to Maryland in 1684. [CLRO]

MORRISEAUX, ..., Cure of Charlebourg, Quebec, 1764. [JCTP.71.455]

MORRISET, PIERRE, a French refugee, landed in Virginia, 1700. [SPAWI.1700.681]

MORVAL, SEBASTIEN, master of St Jean de La Rochelle from La Rochelle to Quebec in 1695. [Charente Maritime Archives, B235, 330-339]

MOSNERON, MATHURIN DESORE, master of Le Fleuron which was captured when bound from the West Indies in 1747. [NA.HCA32.112/1]

MOUCHET, ..., in St Kitts, 1673. [SPAWI.1673.1048]

MOUL, TIMOTHEE, wife and child, French refugees, landed in Virginia, 1700. [SPAWI.1700.681]

MOULIN, ABRAHAM, and wife, French refugees, landed in Virginia, 1700. [SPAWI.1700.681]

MOUNIER, FRANCIS, a merchant in Quebec, 1767. [JCTP.74.181]

MOUNIER, HENRY, a merchant at the Bay of Chaleur, Quebec, 1767; made a Loyalist claim in 1789. [JCTP.74.181][NA.AO13.6.504-507]

MOUNTIGNY, ..., in Newfoundland, 1705. [SPAWI.1705.1185]

MULLON, ESTIENNE JACQUES, master of La Badine a privateer, which was captured when bound for the West Indies in 1745. [NA.HCA32.98/1]

NARCISS, Father, at Louisbourg, Acadia,1728. [SPAWI.1728.395]

NAU, PIERRE, wife and two daughters, French refugees, landed in Virginia, 1700. [SPAWI.1700.681]

NAUDAIN, RAIMOND, master of the L'Expeditif which was captured when bound for the West Indies in 1747. [NA.HCA32.110]

NEALL, FRANCOIS, at Fort William, New York, 1708. [SPAWI.1710.190]

NEGON, ..., Intendant of Canada, 1721, 1722, 1725. [JCTP.1722.362] [SPAWI.1722.73; 1725.740]

NERMAN, Le Marquis, master of Le Monarch at Martinique in 1702. [SPAWI.1702.195]

NESMOND, ..., from Newfoundland to France, 1697. [SPAWI.1697.1393]

NICHOLAUS, ..., a French pirate based in Martinique, master of a sloop with 6 guns and 63 men, 1721. [SPAWI.1721.463iii]

NICOD, ABRAHAM, a French refugee, landed in Virginia, 1700; settled in Mannakin Town, Virginia, by 1701. [SPAWI.1700.681; 1701.1176]

NICOLAY, JACQUES, a French refugee, landed in Virginia, 1700. [SPAWI.1700.681]

NICOLAY, SOUBRAGON, a French refugee, landed in Virginia, 1700. [SPAWI.1700.681]

NOEL, NICOLAS, master of Saint Paul of Quebec from Bordeaux to Quebec and the West Indies in 1689. [Gironde Archives, 6B73/63, 6B294]

The French in the Americas, 1620-1820

NOLLEAU, PHILIPPE, master of La Francoise captured when bound from Newfoundland to France in 1744. [NA.HCA32.111/2]

OGER, JEAN, wife and three children, French refugees, landed in Virginia, 1700. [SPAWI.1700.681]

OGERON, ..., Governor of Tortuga, 1677. [SPAWI.1677.383]

OLIVIE, ..., a planter in Basseterre, St Kitts, before 1704. [SPAWI.1704,221]

ORANGE, LOUIS, wife and child, French refugees, landed in Virginia, 1700. [SPAWI.1700.681]

ORSONAU, CHARLES, master of the L'Eveillee de l'Isle Dieu which was captured when bound from the West Indies in 1746. [NA.HCA32.107/2]

OVERY, ..., in St Kitts, 1672. [SPAWI.1672.903]

PALAIRET, ELIAS JOHN, in Grenada, dead by 1774. [JCTP.1774.390]

PALLOM, ANTHONY, was granted 200 acres in Granville County, South Carolina, 1738. [NA.CO5.398]

PALLOTAN, JOHN BAPTIST, born 1704, a barber from Toulon, bound from London to Pennsylvania as an indentured servant in 1723. [CLRO]

PANETIER, ISAAC, a French refugee, landed in Virginia, 1700. [SPAWI.1700.681]

PANTIER, PIERRE, in Dominica, 1773. [JCTP.1773.334]

PAPILLON, JOSEPH, master of the St Esprit de Quebec, 1774, made a Loyalist claim. [NA.AO13.81.313; AO13.320.327]

PAPILLON, PETER, a merchant in Boston, with cargo aboard the Catherine of Boston forfeited as a pirate vessel in Antigua 1730. [APCCol.1735.292]

PAPIN, GABRIEL, land grant in St Kitts, 1696. [APCCol.1738.417][SPAWI.1715.585iii]

PARADIS, JEAN, master of La Perle from La Rochelle to Quebec in 1698/1699/1700. [Charente Maritime Archives]

The French in the Americas, 1620-1820

PARISE, THERESE, in Dominica, 1772. [JCTP.1772.319]

PARMANTIER, JEAN, a French refugee, landed in Virginia, 1700. [SPAWI.1700.681]

PARRANTOS, JEAN, and sister, French refugees, landed in Virginia, 1700. [SPAWI.1700.681]

PASQUEAN, Captain, master of a sloop, a privateer armed with 4 guns, with 70 men, attacking shipping near the Bahama Islands in 1709. [SPAWI.1709.870]

PATUREAU, LOUIS, and his wife Elizabeth, in South Carolina, depositions, 1734. [SPAWI.1734.161]

PATY, ..., in St Domingo, 1699. [SPAWI.1699.45]

PAULET, PIERRE, master of L'Henriette a privateer which captured when bound for the West Indies in 1745. [NA.HCA32.117]

PAYARD, ELINOR, in Dominica, 1771. [JCTP.1773.248]

PAYARD, PIERRE, in Dominica, 1771. [JCTP.1773.248]

PECHELLS, ..., a French Protestant in St Kitts, 1716. [JCTP.1716.197]

PECHEREA, ..., at St Vincent, 1730. [SPAWI.1730.260iii]

PECY, ..., in Quebec, 1711. [JCTP.1711.673]

PEIRE, MATHEW L., was granted 50 acres in Granville County, South Carolina, 1738. [NA.CO5.398]

PELLETIER, JOHN, in Dominica, 1776. [JCTP.83.13]

PELLETREAUX, ELIAS, a merchant in New York, 1701.[SPAWI.1701.551]

PELLETREAUX, MAGDELENA, in New York, 1701. [SPAWI.1701.138]

PERONEAU, SAMUEL, in Charlestown, Carolina, 1709. [SPAWI.1709.411i]

PERROT, NICOLAS, born 1644, an explorer in Mississippi and Canada, died 1717. [HLF]

The French in the Americas, 1620-1820

PERRUT, PIERRE, and wife, French refugees, landed in Virginia, 1700. [SPAWI.1700.681]

PESCHEUR, JULLIEN, in Martinique licensed to hunt, fish, and cut wood on St Lucia by the Governor of Martinique, 1688. [SPAWI.1688.1718.iii]

PETER, ..., in St Kitts, 1672. [SPAWI.1672.903]

PETER, JOHN, born 1704 in Marseilles, bound from London to Jamaica as an indentured servant in 1723. [CLRO]

PETIT, JEAN BAPTISTE, in Dominica, 1772. [JCTP.1773.280]

PETIT, RENE, the King's Agent at Rouen, petitioned that 80 Huguenot families be transported from London to Carolina, 1679.(they sailed aboard the Richmond, Captain Dunbar) He was, later, granted a manor of 4000 acres there by the Proprietors.
[SPAWI.1679.875/888/918/919/920/930/1000/1006/1149/1167/1233]

PETITPOIS, PAUL, a merchant at Canso, Canada, 1719, 1724. [SPAWI.1719.208ii; 1725.718viii]

PHILIPE, CLAUDE, and wife, French refugees, landed in Virginia, 1700. [SPAWI.1700.681]

PHILIPE, JACQUES, wife and four children, French refugees, landed in Virginia, 1700. [SPAWI.1700.681]

PHILIPPEAUX, ..., Governor of the French Islands of America, at Martinique, 1711; 1714; 1719. [SPAWI.1711.623i; 1714.257/337/480; 1719.394]

PHILIZOT, PHILIP, son of Odo Philizot in Paris, an indentured servant bound from London to Pennsylvania in 1684. [CLRO]

PIAGET, ..., a French army officer who fought the Chickasaw, 1736. [SPAWI.1736.381]

PIERRO, ..., a planter in Fig Tree Quarter, St Kitts, before 1717. [JCTP.1717.261]

The French in the Americas, 1620-1820

PIERRON, JEAN, a Jesuit priest, from La Rochelle on 10 April 1667 bound for Canada, landed on 27 June 1667, at Tionnontogen in September 1667 bound for Orange; at Schnectady on 23 October 1667. [CSPC.1667.1571/1617]

PIKE, ..., an interpreter at Placentia, Newfoundland, 1714. [SPAWI.1715.194x]

PINGAULT, JACQUES, master of the Marie de Brouage from La Rochelle to Newfoundland and Acadia in 1661. [La Rochelle Library, Moreau ms]

PINNELL, ABEL, was granted 50 acres in Granville County, South Carolina, 1738. [NA.CO5.398]

PIQUENOT, PIERRE, master of the privateer Le Roi Assuerus which was captured when bound from the West Indies in 1745. [NA.HCA32.149/3]

PISTOLET, JEAN, of the schooner Romaine de Martinique, at Barbados, 1725. [SPAWI.1725.398]

PITRELLE, FRANCOIS, a French prisoner captured at Canso, Nova Scotia, 1720. [SPAWI.1720.241v]

PLAINE, JAMES, son of Francis Plaine, sometime a merchant in Paris, died in Savanna, Georgia, in September 1798, testament, 23 February 1807, Commissariat of Edinburgh. [NRS.Services of Heirs]

PLAINMARAIS, ..., with his wife Margaret de la Tour, and a daughter, near Annapolis Royal, 1732. [SPAWI.1732.259]

POIGNAUD, JOSEPH, master of La Diamant which was captured when bound from the West Indies in 1745. [NA.HCA32.104/2]

POISSON, Father, killed by the Chicachas at Fort Saint Claude in 1730. [HLF]

POMIER, ..., in Martinique, master of a brigantine seized by the pirate Roberts off St Lucia in October 1721. [SPAWI.1721.501vi]

PONISETT, MARTIN, General Superior of the Jesuit Mission in America, in Martinique, 1688. [SPAWI.1688.1830]

PONTEGRAVE, ..., in St Kitts, 1672. [SPAWI.1672.903]

The French in the Americas, 1620-1820

POSTEL, FELIX, master of La Concorde which was captured when bound from the West Indies in 1745. [NA.HCA32.100/2]

POULET, GUILLAUME, master of St Andre de la Rochelle from La Rochelle to Quebec in 1659. [La Rochelle Library, Moreau.185]

POYETT,....., in St Kitts, 1673. [SPAWI.1673.1048]

PREVILLE, ..., on the River St John, Nova Scotia, son-in-law of Alexander Bourg, 1732. [SPAWI.1732.259]

PREVOST, ADAM, a French refugee, landed in Virginia, 1700. [SPAWI.1700.681]

PREVOST, MARIE, a French refugee, landed in Virginia, 1700. [SPAWI.1700.681]

PRIOLEAU, ELISHA, in South Carolina, 1724. [SPAWI.1724.388i]

PRIOLEAU, Colonel SAMUEL, was granted 3250 acres in Purrysburgh, South Carolina, 20 June 1732. [SPAWI.1734.225]

PRUNEAU, JACQUES, master of the L'Aigle Noir de la Rochelle from la Rochelle to Quebec and the West Indies, 1679. [La Rochelle Municipal Library ms]

PRUNEAU, THOMAS, master of Le Grenade de la Rochelle from France to Quebec in 1698. [Gironde Archives, ms 6B298/B5694]

PUILLION, JACQUES, on Staten Island, New York, 1689. [SPAWI.1689.352]

PYMON, ..., Governor of St Martin, 1736. [SPAWI.1737.20ii]

QUESNEE, PIERRE, a brewer, 'a marrying man', to emigrate to Virginia, 1621. [CSPC.Addenda; Colonial Correspondence, Vol.i,#45]

QUESNELL, FRANCOIS, master of Le Bien Pris, which was captured when bound from Cap Breton in 1744. [NA.HCA32.99/2]

QUITELLE, ..., a creole from Martinique, a sloopmaster, 1729. [SPAWI.1730.58]

RABO, Father, a Jesuit explorer, died in Canada, 1767. [GM.37.524]

RADIGUET, JACQUES, master of L'Expedition which was captured when bound for the West Indies in 1744; master of Le Prophete Elie which was captured when bound from the West Indies in 1748. [NA.HCA32.108/2; 143/1]

RADISSON, PIERRE ESPRIT, in Hudson Bay Company Service, 1683. [SPAWI.1683.2088/2097]

RALE, SEBASTIEN, a French Jesuit at Narantswalk, New England, 1719; at Narantsoak, Quebec, 1722. [SPAWI.1720.578ii; 1722.73; 1723.805][JCTP.1722.362]

RALLE, Father, in Quebec, 1722. [SPAWI.1723.805]

RATEAU, ELIE NICOLAS, master of Le Lion D'Or which was captured when bound from the Mississippi in 1744. [NA.HCA32.127/1]

RAYMOND, ELIE, master of Le Taureau de la Rochelle from France to Quebec in 1663. [La Rochelle Archives]

RAYMOND, ..., a planter at Pensez y Bien, and a property owner in Basse Terre, St Kitts, before 1717. [JCTP.1717.261]

REGNAUD, LOUIS, master of the Benjamin, a privateer, captured when bound from the West Indies in 1744. Regnaud was killed in the action. [NA.HCA32.98/4]

REGNIER, ..., in New Jersey, 1710. [SPAWI.1711.835xxviii]

REGNOLD, ..., master of the Francis of Havre de Grace from St Kitts to London in 1630. [CSPC.V]

REMBERT, PETER, guilty of murdering Captain Peter Simmons, in South Carolina, 1724. [SPAWI.1724.388v]

REMEE, ..., in St Kitts, 1672. [SPAWI.1672.903]

RENAU, FRANCIS, master of the sloop Wiggbox, seized at Montserrat, 1736. [SPAWI.1737.61i]

RENAUD, ..., a military engineer in the West Indies, 1701. [SPAWI.1701.640]

RENAUD, ..., to Antigonish, Nova Scotia, 1720. [SPAWI.1720.241v]

The French in the Americas, 1620-1820

RENOULT, ..., a French Protestant in St Kitts, 1690. [SPAWI.1690.1212]

RENOULT, ELIZABETH, a Huguenot and a planter in St Kitts before 1688; 1714; estates restored in 1715. [JCTP/1712][RPCCol.1715.1225][SPAWI.1714.631; 1715.375]

RENOULT, Mrs, with four daughters, in St Kitts, 1714, 1717. [JCTP.1717.208] [SPAWI.1714.631/662]

RENOULT, Mrs, from France, in St Kitts, 1729. [SPAWI.1730.58]

RENOULT, Miss, from Martinique to St Domingo in 1729. [SPAWI.1730.58]

REQUIEM, JEAN, master of the Columbe de la Rochelle from La Rochelle to Quebec in 1696. [La Rochelle Archives]

RICHARD, JACQUES, and wife, French refugees, landed in Virginia, 1700. [SPAWI.1700.681]

RICHARDS, MICHAEL, a French inhabitant of Annapolis Royal, Nova Scotia, a deposition, 24 August 1720. [SPAWI.1720.241vii]

RICHARDS, RENY, a farmer near Annapolis Royal, Nova Scotia, 1734. [SPAWI.1734.164i]

RIEUSSET, JOHN, in North Carolina, 1752. [JCTP.1752.297]

RIGUER, NICHOLAS, was granted 200 acres in Granville County, South Carolina, 1738. [NA.CO5.398]

RIVIER, PIERRE, master of Jean of Bordeaux, arrived in Maryland in 1695. [SPAWI.1699/597]

RIVIERE, MAGDALEINE, in St Vincent's, 1777. [JCTP.84.69/100]

ROBARD, JEAN LAURENT, master of Les Bons Enfants which was captured when bound from the West Indies in 1744. [NA.HCA32.98/2]

ROBISHEAU, PRODANE, senior, of the River of Annapolis Royal, Nova Scotia, 1731. [SPAWI.1734.164i]

ROBBILLARD, N., master of the L'Armes de la Compagnie de la Rochelle, from La Rochelle to Canada in 1690. [Charente Maritime Archives]

ROBICHEAU, PRUDENT, a French inhabitant of Annapolis Royal, Nova Scotia, a deposition, 24 August 1720. [SPAWI.1720.241vi]

ROBINS, JACQUES, at Miramachi Bay, Gulf of the St Lawrence, 1763. [JCTP.1764.203

ROBISHEAU, or NIGAN, FRANCIS, at Annapolis Royal, Nova Scotia, 1734. [SPAWI.1734.164i]

ROBISHEAUX, PRUDANE, at Annapolis Royal, Nova Scotia, 1734. [SPAWI.1734.164v]

ROCHEBLAVE, PHILLIPPE, at Fort Gage on the Mississippi, 1776. [NA.AO12.55.129; AO12.70.17; AO12.109.266; AO13.58.261; AO13.92.323; AO13.102.1]

RODOT, ..., Intendant of Canada, 1708. [SPAWI.1708.60]

ROGER, JEAN, a French refugee, landed in Virginia, 1700. [SPAWI.1700.681]

ROLLEAU, PIERRE, master of a 70 ton barque L'Ortolont , bound from Martinique to France, 1704. [SPAWI.1704. 585]

ROMAIN, JOHN, master of the sloop Two Sisters seized at sea on a voyage from St Eustatius to Guadaloupe, and taken to Montserrat, 1736. [SPAWI.1737.61i/658]

ROMBOUTS, FRANCOIS, in New York, 1687. [SPAWI.1687.1250]

ROMVELLE, ..., in Quebec, 1711. [JCTP.1711.673]

RONER, ANDRE, promoter of Swiss emigration to South Carolina, 1722. [SPAWI.1722.378]

ROSE MAONQ, Captain, master of Le Vingeur at Martinique, 1702. [SPAWI.1702.195]

ROSIE, JEAN, from Canada to Albany, New York, 1687. [SPAWI.1687.1421]

The French in the Americas, 1620-1820

ROUBAUD, PETER, a former Jesuit in Canada, sent to England by General Murray, a memorial to the king, 30 May 1770. [Cal.HOP.1770/163]

ROUX, JACQUES CHARLES, master of L'Intrepide which was captured when bound from the West Indie in 1744. [NA.HCA32.118/1]

ROUX, MICHAEL, a French refugee, landed in Virginia, 1700. [SPAWI.1700.681]

ROY, DANIEL, a French refugee, landed in Virginia, 1700. [SPAWI.1700.681]

ROY, JACQUES, and wife, French refugees, landed in Virginia, 1700. [SPAWI.1700.681]

SAGE, JAN, a Walloon serge maker, with his wife and six children, to emigrate to Virginia, 1621. [CSPC.Addenda; Colonial Correspondence, Vol.i,#45]

SAGE, PHILLIPE, master of Saint Phillipe de Bordeaux from Bordeaux to Quebec and the West Indies in 1687 and 1688; master of Le Sage de Bordeaux from France to Quebec in 1689; from Bordeaux to Quebec and the West Indies in 1691. [Bordeaux Archives, Loste ms251, Cazenove; Gironde Archives, 6B72/73, 165, 6B75/17, 6B294/31, 6B295/220]

SAGRAN, ..., French agent in St Eustatia, 1737. [SPAWI.1737.318]

SAINT ALBAN, ..., a French subject in St Kitts, 1688. [APCCol.1733.259]

SAINT AMOUR, Sieur HENRY, in Martinique licensed to hunt, fish, and cut wood on St Lucia by the Governor of Martinique, 1688. [SPAWI.1688.1718.i]

SAINT BLANHAIRE, ..., a French soldier captured in Canada, 1759. [SM.21.541]

SAINT CLEMENS, JOHN, a native of France residing in Barbados, was granted denization in 1671. [SPAWI.1671.411]

SAINT DENNY, ..., in St Kitts, 1672. [SPAWI.1672.903]

SAINT DU PUY, JOSEPH ALLAIN FROMY, master of Le Postillion de St Malo which was captured when bound for the West Indies in 1746. [NA.HCA32.145]

SAINT LAURENCE, ..., Governor of Guadaloupe, 1671. [SPAWI.1671.508]

The French in the Americas, 1620-1820

SAINT LEON, ..., Governor of Guadaloupe, 1674. [SPAWI.1674.1333]

SAINT MARC, PIERRE, master of the Recontre de la Rochelle from France to Quebec and the West Indies in 1689. [La Rochelle Archives, Berthelot ms]

SAINT MARKE, ..., in St Kitts, 1672. [SPAWI.1672.903]

SAINT MARTIN,........, Governor of St Lucia, 1719. [SPAWI.1719.384/404/411/422/439/469/505]

SAINT OVIDE, ..., on Cape Breton Island. [SPAWI.1719.208ii]

SAINT SANRESIS, Chevalier, in St Kitts, 1678. [SPAWI.1678.741.ix]

SALENAVE, ... a planter on St Kitts before 1712. [JCTP.1716.180]

SALES, FRANCIS, a French Indian at St John's River, Nova Scotia, 1720. [SPAWI.1720.241x]

SALINAVE, ELIZABETH, a French Protestant in St Kitts, 1690, 1714, 1715. [SPAWI.1690.1212; 1714.619/628/630xi/xiv/662; 1715.147i]

SALVAGE, Sieur, at Montreal, 1683. [SPAWI.1683.1201]

SALVER, PERIER, a French naval commander, 1756. [APCCol.1756.324]

SALVETAT, PETER, a planter in St Kitts, 1723. [SPAWI.1723.532]

SANCE, Baron de, proposed to recruit 100 men from amongst Protestant families in France and England to settle in Carolina, 1630. [CSPCol.V]

SANS-CHAGRIN, ..., a soldier, killed by the Chicachas at Fort Saint Claude in 1730. [HLF]

SANSON, JACQUES, master of La Catherine which was captured when bound from the West Indies in 1745. [NA.HCA32.103/1]

SANS-SOUCY, ..., a soldier, killed by the Chicachas at Fort Saint Claude in 1730. [HLF]

SARDIN, SIMON, a French refugee, landed in Virginia, 1700. [SPAWI.1700.681]

The French in the Americas, 1620-1820

SARGENTON, JEAN, wife and child, French refugees, landed in Virginia, 1700. [SPAWI.1700.681]

SASSIN, FRANCOIS, a French refugee, landed in Virginia, 1700. [SPAWI.1700.681]

SAUIN, JEAN, a French refugee, landed in Virginia, 1700. [SPAWI.1700.681]

SAURIN, PIERRE, master of the Saint Andre of Leogone, Hispaniola, at New Providence, 1736. [SPAWI.1736.454]

SAVOY, JAIRMAINT, a French inhabitant at the Annapolis River, Nova Scotia, 1720. [SPAWI.1720.180xvii]

SAYE, JEAN, a French refugee, landed in Virginia, 1700. [SPAWI.1700.681]

SEBASTIEN DE L'ESPERANCE, CHARLES GABRIEL, Governor of St Pierre and Miquelon, 1773 to 1778, and from 1783 to 1785.

SEHEUT, TERTULIEN, wife and two children, French refugees, landed in Virginia, 1700. [SPAWI.1700.681]

SENE, MARGUERITE, and daughter, French refugees, landed in Virginia, 1700. [SPAWI.1700.681]

SERRE, NOAH, in South Carolina, 1724; was granted 500 acres in Craven County, South Carolina, 1737. [SPAWI.1724.388i][NA.CO5.398]

SEVERIN, JOHN, planter in St Kitts, from 1686. [SPAWI.1690.1124/1125/1177/1178]

SHEM, NOELL, from Burgundy, an indentured servant bound for Bristol to Barbados in 1657. [Bristol Record Office]

SIBERON, ANDRE, master of Le Neptune de la Rochelle from La Rochelle to Acadia in 1666. [Charente Maritime Archives, B5671.184]

SIBERON, ELIE, master of La Paix from La Rochelle to Quebec in 1664. [Charente Maritime Archives, B5665]

SIERS, PAUL, a resident of New Brunswick, 1786. [NA.AO13.80.325]

SIERS, PIERRE, a resident of New Brunswick, 1786. [NA.AO13.80.325]

SIGNAC, PETER, a merchant in Placentia, Newfoundland, 1723, 1730. [JCTP.1723.32][SPAWI.1723.491a; 1730.422iva]

SIGOURNEY, ANDREW, a distiller in Boston, 1720. [SPAWI.1720.22i]

SIRESME, JACQUES, a Jesuit priest among the Abnaquis, New England, 1731. [SPAWI.1731.12]

SIVERET, PHILLIPE, master of the Jeanne bound for Pentagouet, Acadia, when seized by the English at Pemaquid, 1687. [SPAWI.1687.1492/1545/1560/1592/1595/1608/1615/2150]

SOBLET, ABRAHAM, and two children, French refugees, landed in Virginia, 1700. [SPAWI.1700.681]

SOUBIRA, JEAN LOUIS, master of the La Belle Judith captured when bound from the West Indies to France in 1747. [NA.HCA32.98/1]

SOUBRAS, ..., on Cape Breton Island, 1719. [SPAWI.1719.208ii]

SOUKEUR, ..., in Onnandage, New York, 1701. [SPAWI.1701.

SOULEGRE, PETER, a planter on St Kitts, 1712, 1714, 1717, 1719, 1723, 1729, co-owner of the frigate St Christopher before the Admiralty Court of the Leeward Islands 3 January 1719; Councillor of St Kitts, 1724, in London by 1737. [JCTP.1717.260; 1729.16/21/103/366][SPAWI.1714.678II; 1723.531/772; 1729.632/633/1035; 1737.55iii] [APCCol.1719.1316]

SUGRE, JACQUES, a French refugee, landed in Virginia, 1700. [SPAWI.1700.681]

SURVILLE, JEAN, master of La Bagatelle captured when bound for the West Indies in 1747. [NA.HCA32.98/1]

TABERY, ..., in St Kitts, 1672. [SPAWI.1672.903]

TACHET, ..., was granted St Maudet, Quebec, 16 May 1763. [JCTP.71.449; 74.137]

The French in the Americas, 1620-1820

TADOURNEAU, ELIE, master of Le Taureau de la Rochelle from La Rochelle to Quebec in 1656 and 1657. [La Rochelle Archives]

TANQUERAY, ESTIENNE, master of Le Charles Vincent a French Newfoundland fisheries ship which was captured in 1744. [NA.HCA32.102/1]

TANQUERAY, JACQUES, master of Le Caesar a French Newfoundland fisheries ship which was captured in 1744. [NA.HCA32.103/1]

TANQUET, JACQUES, master of Sainte Anne de St Malo from Newfoundland bound for St Malo in 1673. [APCCol.1674.975]

TAPIN, JACQUES, master of Le Comte de Carbonnel which was captured when bound for the Newfoundland fisheries in 1747. [NA.HCA32.103/2]

TARDIEU, JEAN, a French refugee, landed in Virginia, 1700. [SPAWI.1700.681]

TAUREAU, GABRIEL, in Dominica, 1772. [JCTP.1772.319]

TELLIER, ..., in St Kitts, 1672. [SPAWI.1672.903]

TERRIOT, PIERRE, resident of Minnes, Nova Scotia, 1718. [SPAWI.1718.371iv]

THARAY, PIERRE, master of the Saint Charles from La Rochelle to Acadia in 1682. [Charente Maritime Archives, B5681]

THAUVET, Captain ANDREW, a French Protestant and planter in St Kitts, 1696, 1715. [JCTP.1716.197][SPAWI.1715.585; 1716/432; 1731.505] [APCCol.1738.417]

THIBOU, ESTHER, from Antigua, married George Blount in London on 2 January 1753. [GM.23.51]

THIBOU, ISAAC, in Antigua, 1739. [APCCol.1739.484]

THIBOU, JACOB, a planter and merchant in Antigua, 1708, 1718, 1728. [SPAWI.1709.150.XI,484xxvi; 1718.413] [APCCol.1729.177]

THOMAS, JACQUE, master of Le Hector de St Malo a privateer which was captured when bound from the West Indies in 1747. [NA.HCA32.116/2]

THOMAS, JEAN, master of <u>Catherine de la Rochelle</u> from La Rochelle to Canada and the West Indies in 1695. [Charente Maritime Archives, B5691]

THOMAS, JACQUES, master of <u>Jean de Chaillevette</u> from La Rochelle to Quebec in 1691. [Charente Maritime Archives, B235]

THOMAS, JEAN, master of the <u>Catherine de la Rochelle</u> from La Rochelle to Canada and the West Indies, 1695. [Charente Maritime Archives, B5691]

THOMAS, JEAN MICHEL, master of <u>La Charmante Susanne</u> a privateer which was captured when bound for Cayenne in 1747. [NA.HCA32.102/1]

THOMAS, PIERRE, master of <u>Le Plaisir de la Rochelle</u> from La Rochelle to Acadia in 1664; master of <u>Le Postillon de la Rochelle</u> from La Rochelle to Quebec and the West Indies in 1673; from France to Quebec in 1693. [La Rochelle Archives, Moreau, 27; Riviere and Soulard] [Charente Maritime Archives, B5672/3]

THOMAS, SAMUEL, master of the <u>Anne Marie de la Rochelle</u> from France to Quebec in 1698. [Gironde Archives ms]

TIGNAC, ELIZABETH, a French refugee, landed in Virginia, 1700. [SPAWI.1700.681]

TILLON, PIERRE, a French refugee, landed in Virginia, 1700. [SPAWI.1700.681]

TITRE, GEORGE, in Dominica, 1773. [JCTP.1773.334]

TITRE, LEWIS JOSEPH, in Dominica, 1773. [JCTP.1773.334]

TORAILLES, Sieur, a prisoner in Barbados, 1704. [SPAWI.1704.666/888]

TOURNEAU, JEAN, master of <u>Saint Joseph de la Rochelle</u> from La Rochelle to Quebec in 1666. [La Rochelle Archives, Teuleron/Cherbonnier]

TRAHEU, JOSEPH, born in France, a Spanish subject in Puerto Rico, 1730. [SPAWI.1730.602]

TRAVERSIER, MICHAEL, in Dominica, 1772. [JCTP.1773.280]

TREJUSSON, ELIE, and wife, French refugees, landed in Virginia, 1700. [SPAWI.1700.681]

The French in the Americas, 1620-1820

TREMBLANT, ..., on St Vincent, 1728. [SPAWI.1730.260vii]

TRESNEAU, ANDREW, in New York, co-owner of the Rhode Island built sloop Good Intent, 1717. [JCTP.1717.437]

TRISTRANT, SIMON, from St Thomas, West Indies, to South Carolina, 1701. [SPAWI.1701.180]

TROILLARDE, ANTHOINE, a French refugee, landed in Virginia, 1700. [SPAWI.1700.681]

TRUYBER, HELEN, a French refugee, landed in Virginia, 1700. [SPAWI.1700.681]

TULON, GARANTRE, from St Malo, France, aboard the St Elina Modesta of St Malo bound for Cape Breton, landed there 2 May 1715. [SPAWI.1716.47]

TULON LA GARANDERIE, OLIVIER, a fisherman at St Pierre, Newfoundland, trading with Bilbao, 1716, 1717, 1718. [JCTP.1716.214][SPAWI.1717.468i/491; 1718.318]

VA DE BON COEUR, ..., a soldier, killed by the Chicachas at Fort Saint Claude in 1730. [HLF]

VALER,......, killed by the Chicachas at Fort Saint Claude in 1730. [HLF]

VALLIANT, FRANCOIS, a Jesuit missionary in Canada, 1687. [SPAWI.1687.1421/1566/1638]

VALIERE, PIERRE, in Quebec, a deposition, 1763. [JCTP.1763.308]

VALOURS, JACQUES, was granted 200 acres in Granville County, South Carolina, 1738. [NA.CO5.398]

VANDRUEIL, Marquis de, Governor of Quebec, 1705, 1718, 1719, 1720. [JCTP.1706.263; 1718.36; 1719.64/80; 1720.217; 1722.362]

VAUDREVILLE, ..., Governor of Louisiana, a letter,1749. [JCTP.1750.65]

VAUGUELIN, JEAN CHARLES, master of Le Mentor which was captured when bound from the West Indies in 1744. [NA.HCA32.131/1]

The French in the Americas, 1620-1820

VAUQUELLIN, alias DE LA PRAIRIE, ROBERT, born 1624 in Caen, Normandy, land surveyor of New Jersey by 1674. [NA.HCA.Carteret v.Idle, 1674]

VAUSSAUGES, CHARLES, master of Le Roi David which was captured when bound for Cayenne in 1747. [NA.HCA32.148/2]

VERDIER, ANDRE, was granted 500 acres in Granville County, South Carolina, 1738. [NA.CO5.398]

VERGNIAN, Captain, master of L'Infante de la Rochelle at Acadia in 1677. [Charente Maritime Archives]

VERNAYS, FRANCIS, was granted 50 acres in Granville County, South Carolina, 1738. [NA.CO5.398]

VERON, CLAUDE, master of Le Rubis which was captured when bound from the West Indies in 1744. [NA.HCA32.149/1]

VERON, JACQUES, and wife, French refugees, landed in Virginia, 1700. [SPAWI.1700.681]

VERRY, ISAAC, a French refugee, landed in Virginia, 1700. [SPAWI.1700.681]

VEYREL, ISAAC, a French Protestant, petitioned to be shipped to America, possibly went to Jamaica, 1682. [SPAWI.1682.883]

VEYRES, JEAN MATHIEU, master of La Diligente which was captured when bound for Havana in 1745. [NA.HCA.104/2]

VEYRIERR, MICHAEL NATHANIEL, in Dominica, 1771. [JCTP.1773.274]

VEYSSIERE, JEAN BAPTISTE NOEL, educated in seminaries in Quebec and France, a missionary to the Iroquois, a former Recollet priest who converted to Protestantism, around 1767, appointed Anglican minister at Trois Rivieres. [FPA#8/325]

VIDAN, JEAN, a French refugee, landed in Virginia, 1700. [SPAWI.1700.681]

VIGOREUX, ISAAC, from La Rochelle, from London to Pennsylvania, 1684. [LMWB.13/502]

The French in the Americas, 1620-1820

VIGNEAU, PIERRE, master of Marie de Bordeaux, from Bordeaux to Quebec in 1698. [Gironde Archives. 6B10191]

VIGNES, ADAM, a French refugee, landed in Virginia, 1700. [SPAWI.1700.681]

VILLAR, Captain, master of Le Biguare at Martinique in 1702. [SPAWI.1702.195]

VILLEBONNE, ..., Governor of Acadia, at Port Royal, 1689. [SPAWI.1691.1857]

VILLEPONTOUX, PETER, in South Carolina, 1724. [SPAWI.1724.388i]

VILLEROY, ..., a vagabond and thief, near Fort Orange, 1683. [SPAWI.1683.1201]

VINCENT, MARIE ELIZABETH, in St Vincent's, 1777. [JCTP.84.69/100]

VINCENT, Father, priest of Chignecto, 1720. [SPAWI.1720.241vi]

VISSE-BRAS,........, a soldier, killed by the Chicachas at Fort Saint Claude in 1730. [HLF]

VITTET, JEAN BAPTISTE, on St Vincent, 1777. [JCTP.84.117]

VITRY, DENYS, pilot at Cape Gaspe, Quebec, a memorial, 1764. [JCTP.1764.214/222]

VIVEGNIS, ..., proposed to establish a colony in Florida, 1764. [JCTP.71.413]

VIVIER, MARTIN, master of La Catherine de Bordeaux captured when bound from the West Indies in 1747. [NA.HCA32.101/1]

VOLLARD, PETRE, in Antigua, 1709. [SPAWI.1709.487ii]

VOYES, JACQUES, a French refugee, landed in Virginia, 1700. [SPAWI.1700.681]

WAUTRE, GEORGE, a musician, with his wife and four children, to emigrate to Virginia, 1621. [CSPC.Addenda; Colonial Correspondence, Vol.i,#45]

www.ingramcontent.com/pod-product-compliance
Lightning Source LLC
Chambersburg PA
CBHW071223160426
43196CB00012B/2402